CENTRAL FISHERIES BOARD
IRISH ANGLING GUIDES

Coarse Angling

GILL AND MACMILLAN

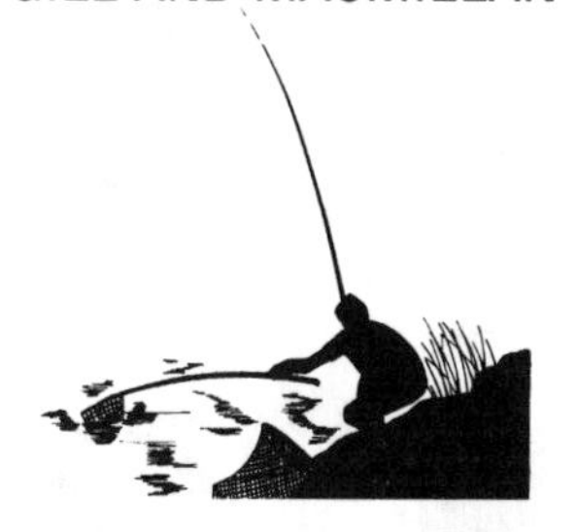

Gill and Macmillan Ltd
Goldenbridge
Dublin 8
with associated companies throughout the world
www.gillmacmillan.ie

0 7171 1826 6
Editorial Consultant Roberta Reeners
Design and Artwork by Design Image, Dublin
Print origination by Seton Music Graphics Ltd, Bantry, Co. Cork
Printed in Malaysia
The maps are based on the Ordnance Survey by permission of the Government
(Permit No. 5552)

A catalogue record is available for this book from the British Library.

2 4 6 5 3

COARSE ANGLING

CENTRAL FISHERIES BOARD
IRISH ANGLING GUIDES

A totally comprehensive series of handbooks on every aspect of angling in Ireland. Compiled by and published in association with the Irish Fisheries Boards, each Guide provides all the most recent and accurate information required by the angler to make the most of Ireland's superb angling opportunities.

The series comprises three books:
Sea Angling
Coarse Angling
Game Angling

THE FISHERIES BOARDS

The Central and seven Regional Fisheries Boards were established to protect, develop and promote all forms of sport fishing in Ireland. They are non-profit-making bodies and all income, including the royalties from this book, is devoted to fishery improvement and conservation. The Central Board employs specialist Coarse, Game and Sea angling staff whose main function is the collection and dissemination of angling information such as is included here.

The Board wishes to thank its colleagues all over the country, the thousands of anglers, the boat operators, club secretaries, fishery owners and all those interested and involved in the sport without whose co-operation these guides could not be produced.

INFORMATION

The nature of angling is such that the information provided must be viewed as being as accurate as possible at the time of going to print.

The Fisheries Boards provide maps, brochures and some local guides, and Bord Failte, the Irish Tourist Board, provides a set of three brochures titled 'Only The Best' Coarse, Game and Sea Angling.

The Irish Tourist Board also inspects accommodation, registering and approving only the premises meeting its high standards. The Fisheries Boards recommend that anglers stay only at such approved accommodation. Guides and lists are available from any tourist office.

CONTENTS

COUNTY LIST

MAJOR COARSE FISHING LOCATIONS

INTRODUCTION

Ireland is an island of about 32,000 square miles (82,880 km^2), situated on a shallow shelf in the North Atlantic. The island is 189 miles (304 km) wide and its greatest length measures 302 miles (486 km).

The interior of Ireland is, in general, flat with the mountains following, more or less, the lines of the sea coast. The centre of the island, in which a lot of the coarse fish waters are to be found, is almost entirely of limestone. In the north midlands, the formation is superficially different, but even here the limestone is present, although for the most part it is deeply buried. Many lakes and streams have their origins in springs coming up from a great depth. There are also limestone deposits washed down into the small rivers which in turn feed the larger waters. The presence of lime in large quantities results in characteristics caused by no other geological formation.

Ireland's natural environment is the envy of Europe. The waters here are the cleanest in Europe and the Irish countryside never suffered the ravages of an industrial revolution. The waters are uncrowded and anglers can enjoy their fishing in peace and quiet in a pleasant countryside.

The typical coarse fish water is likely to have reeds, sedges and water lilies. The water itself will almost certainly be alkaline. Such conditions result in great quantities of food being available to the fish: tubifex worms, blood worms, ascellus (fresh water louse), chironomid larvae, caddis, snail and fresh water shrimp.

One of the great attractions to Irish coarse fishing waters is the variety that they offer anglers – slow moving and fast rivers, big fish-filled lakes to small, friendly ponds which one can fish on calm days. Canals and small rivers also produce great sport throughout the year. There are also those waters which seldom, if ever, see an angler and where one can become a true explorer.

Bream abound in most coarse fishing waters and Roach are now to be found in most, but not all, areas. Great sport can be had with fighting Hybrids, Rudd, Perch, Tench, Dace and Pike. Just two or three lakes hold Carp in Ireland.

The coarse fishing waters are monitored on a regular basis by the Fisheries Boards and are being surveyed to obtain information for anglers. For more than twenty years, state agencies, in conjunction with local angling and tourist organisations, have been developing facilities on their waters. Access to waters from roadside car parks is over stiles and footbridges. In most cases, anglers fish on good, clean banks; but if the margins are reeded, fishing stands are provided. The waters are well signposted and the Fisheries Boards have provided angling maps and brochures to make it easy to find the fishing.

The coarse fishing season extends over the whole year. There is no close season for coarse fish here. The coarse angler in Ireland can enjoy great sport for Roach, which feed at most times because of our mild climate. Bream fishing from March can extend up to the first light frost in November. Summer temperatures can rise to 25°C and our waters are seldom frozen in the winter. Pike fishing also extends over the year; it is only the catching techniques which change from season to season. Big Pike are common in our large and deep lakes. Anglers should always be aware of the danger from winds which can rise quickly. Always take care on big lakes and wear life saving gear.

As many of Irish coarse fishing waters, especially in the early season, are seldom fished, it is essential to ground bait swims heavily and wait. Do not ramble on to another water, but remain at the pre-baited swim and give it a chance.

New clubs/associations are continually being formed and new fisheries are being developed on an ongoing basis. These will appear in the next edition.

■ ANGLING FESTIVALS

Angling festivals are now part of the Irish angling scene. Festivals take place at many centres from about Easter to October on a variety of waters. The format is mostly the same all over, with anglers fishing about four waters over a week.

Prize money is good, and with pools and trophies, anglers can be well rewarded. Top stars, including world champions, are attracted to our Irish festivals, but the magic of Irish waters will often help unknown anglers to take the top prizes.

Irish festivals are popular, not only because they produce great catches of fish, but friendships are cultivated, bringing anglers back year after year. Anglers will always find the warmth of that Irish welcome when they arrrive at the Irish guesthouse.

Information on competitions is available from the Central and Regional Fisheries Boards and the Irish Tourist Board. A useful list of matches is published by the National Coarse Fishing Federation. Details of competitions will also be available from local tourist organisations and your local travel agent.

APRIL

Bailieborough. Contact Mrs Shiela Kelly, Bailieborough, Co. Cavan, Tel (042) 65361.

Castleblayney. Contact Leisure Angling, Liverpool, Tel (051) 734 2344.

MAY

Mullingar. Contact Sam Smyth, Castle Street, Mullingar, Tel (044) 40431.

Carrickmacross. Contact Mrs Nuala Russell, Nurebeg House, Carrickmacross, Co. Monaghan, Tel (042) 61044.

Prosperous. Contact Mrs Anne Clarke, Downings, Prosperous, Co. Kildare, Tel (045) 60187.

Carlow & Graiguecullen. Contact I. Hutchinson, 46 Beechwood Park, Carlow, Tel (0503) 39592.

Ballinasloe. Contact Mr J.A. Ellis, 23 Ard Mhuire, Ballinasloe, Co. Galway, Tel (0905) 42668, or emergency number Pat Lawless, Tel (0905) 42512.

Enfield. Contact Mr Michael Boyle, Kilshanroe, Enfield, Co. Meath, Tel (0405) 41356.

Ballybay. Contact Joe McNally, Lake Lodge House, Ballybay, (042) 41114.

MAY/JUNE

Edenderry. Contact Leisure Angling, 33 Dovedale Road, Liverpool L18 5EP; or John Colgan, Bella Vista, St Mary's Road, Edenderry, Co. Offaly, Tel (0405) 31179.

Fermoy. Contact Mr Norman Berry, Corrin View, Fermoy, Co. Cork, Tel (025) 32074.

JULY

Athlone. Contact Mr Jim Denby, Shelmalier House, Retreat Road, Athlone, Co. Westmeath, Tel (0902) 72245.

Belturbet. Contact Anthony Vesey, O'Reilly Garage, Belturbet, Tel (049) 22104.

Drumconrath. Contact Mrs A . Ward, Inis Fail, Drumconrath, Co. Meath, Tel (041) 54161.

SEPTEMBER

Limerick. European Pike Championship. Contact Jim Robinson, Thomond Shopping Centre, Tel (061) 44900.

Arva. Contact Eamonn Grey, Breffni Arms, Arva, Tel (049) 35127.

Cootehill. Contact Secretary, Cootehill Tourist Development, Cootehill, Co. Cavan, Tel (049) 52150 or (049) 52307.

Monaghan. Pairs – Castleblayney/Ballybay.
Contact Del Wilson, Bree, Castleblayney, Tel (042) 46217.

OCTOBER

Athlone. Contact Mr Jim Denby, Shelmalier House, Retreat Road, Athlone, Co. Westmeath, Tel (0902) 72245.

Maggots, worms and pure breadcrumb pre-packed ground bait can be delivered to any of the festivals if ordered in advance, by Irish Angling Services, Ardlougher, Co. Cavan, Tel (049) 26258.

■ THE IRISH KING OF CLUBS ANGLING CHAMPIONSHIP

SEPTEMBER

A fabulous championship for club anglers. Many cash prizes to be won from a prize fund of over IR£10,000. First prize is over IR£3,000 and of course, there are additional trophies and attractive pools. Information from any Irish Tourist Board or B & I office.

English entries for this great competition to King of Clubs, c/o B & I Line, East Princess Dock, Liverpool L3 0AA.

Irish entries contact Robert Buick, 7 Knockvale Grove, Belfast BT5 6HI.

BAIT

Popular ingredients such as crushed barley, bran, maize meal, pollard etc. may be obtained at some centres should you wish to mix your own groundbait. Specially prepared fine breadcrumb groundbait, prepacked, and hook bait (maggots, worms) are available, however, from a network of bait stockists through the country. It may be best to purchase from them or direct from Irish Angling Services Ltd, Ardlougher, Co. Cavan, Tel (049) 26258 which supplies them. Advance ordering is recommended.

LIST OF IRISH ANGLING SERVICES BAIT STOCKISTS

Killeshandra McMahons Gun Shop, Main Street. Tel (049) 34438.

Belturbet McMahons Hardware, Bridge Street. Tel (049) 22400.

Belturbet Mrs Dunne, Hilltop Farm, Kilduff. Tel (049) 22114.

Belturbet Mrs Carol Braiden, Kilduff House, Kilduff. Tel (049) 22452.

Butlersbridge Mrs Mundy, Deredis. Tel (049) 31427.

Cavan Sportsworld, Main Street. Tel (049) 31812.

Cavan Mrs Brady, Lakevilla, Killykeen Area. Tel (049) 31513.

Cavan Mrs Iris Neill, Lisnamandra Farm House, Crossdoney. Tel (049) 37196.

Cloverhill Mrs Smith, Drumbran. Tel (049) 38185.

Cootehill Mr C. Fay, Cabragh House, Cavan Road. Tel (049) 52153.

Carrickmacross Mr Jim McMahon, Carrick Sports Shop. Tel (042) 61714.

Castleblayney Del Wilson, Hill View, Bree. Tel (042) 46217.

Bailieborough McElwaines, Main Street. Tel (042) 65032.

Virginia Mr Ray Arnold, Main Street. Tel (049) 47060.

Carrigallen Jack O'Neill and Son, Main Street. Tel (049) 39738.

Arva Eamonn Grey, Breffni Arms. Tel (049) 35127.

Gowna Mrs F. Kinkade, Lakeside. Tel (043) 83242.

Mohill John Maloney, Glebe House. Tel (078) 31086.
Ballinamore Mrs Elderton, Main Street. Tel (078) 44080.
Boyle Mr Martin Mitchell, Abbey House. Tel (079) 62385.
Drumshanbo/Keshcarrigan, Lough Scur Bait and Tackle, Kilclare. Tel (078) 41438.
Carrick-on-Shannon The Creel, Main Street. Tel (078) 20166.
Carrick-on-Shannon Aisleigh House, Dublin Road. Tel (078) 20313.
Roosky, Bill Boulton, Credit Union House, Dromod.
Tarmonbarry Mr Barry Keenan, Shannon Side House. Tel (043) 26052.
Lanesborough Mrs Holmes, Lakeside Store, Main Street. Tel (043) 21491.
Ballinasloe Mr B. Burton, Woodlands, Dublin Road. Tel (0905) 43123.
Galway Tommy Kavanagh, Cloonabinnia House, Moycullen, Tel (091) 85512.
Shannon Bridge Mr Dermot Killeen, Main Street. Tel (0905) 74112.
Athlone Mr Don Egan, Shannon Side House, West Lodge Road. Tel (0902) 94773.
Naas/Prosperous Countryman Angling, Pacelli Road, Naas. Tel (045) 76047.
Dublin Mr Rory Harkin, 17a Temple Bar. Tel (01) 772351.
Mullingar O'Malleys Fishing Tackle Shop, 33 Dominick Street. Tel (044) 48300.
Tullamore The Tackle Shop, Rahan. Tel (0506) 55979.
Athy Griffin Hawe Ltd, 22 Duke Street. Tel (0509) 31575.
Vicarstown Mr J. Crean, Vicarstown Inn. Tel (0502) 25189.
Carlow John Boyds, Motor & Sport, Tullow Street.
Graiguenamanagh Michael McCabe, Brandon View House, Ballyogan. Tel (0503) 24191.
Portumna Bertie Cummins, Meelick. Tel (0905) 75205. Mr Owen O'Carroll, Oak Park Lodge. Tel (0509) 47143.

Limerick Mr Joe Maloney, Riverside, O'Brien's Bridge, Nr Limerick. Tel. (061) 377303.
Fermoy Mr Jack O'Sullivan, 4 Patrick Street. Tel (025) 31110.
Cappoquin Mrs Flynn, River View House, Cook Street. Tel (058) 54073.
Ballyconnell Barry Nicholson, Irish Angling Services, Co. Cavan. Tel (049) 26258.

THE WATERSIDE CODE OF BEHAVIOUR FOR FISHERMEN

FOLLOW THESE RULES

- Leave no litter. Discarded tackle kills.
- Never cross lands that are not sign-posted and that have no fishing structures.
- When in doubt, ask permission to cross lands.
- Do not drive cars into fields.
- Do not cross meadows. Always walk along the waterside.
- Close all gates and light no fires.
- Respect the landowner's property.

Special Notes

- We stress that you leave no litter. Gather up the plastic bags, the fishing line, the bait bags and bring them home.
- Look out – look up! Do not fish near overhead electricity cables.

USEFUL ADDRESSES

FISHERIES DEPARTMENTS, BOARDS AND NATIONAL ORGANISATIONS

Department of the Marine
Fisheries Administration
Leeson Lane, Dublin 2
Tel (01) 785444.
Abbotstown Laboratories
Tel (01) 210111

Central Fisheries Board
Balnagowan House, Mobhi Boreen,
Glasnevin, Dublin 9
Tel (01) 379206/7/8/9

REGIONAL FISHERIES BOARDS

Eastern Regional Fisheries Board
Balnagowan House
Mobhi Boreen
Glasnevin
Dublin 9
Tel (01) 379209

Southern Regional Fisheries Board
Anglesea Street
Clonmel
Co. Tipperary
Tel (052) 23624

South Western Regional Fisheries Board
1 Nevilles Terrace
Masseytown
Macroom
Co. Cork
Tel (026) 41221/41222

Shannon Regional Fisheries Board
Thomond Weir
Limerick
Tel (061) 55171

Western Regional Fisheries Board
The Weir Lodge
Earl's Island
Galway
Tel (091) 63118/63119/63110

North Western Regional Fisheries Board
Ardnaree House
Abbey Street
Ballina
Co. Mayo
Tel (096) 22623

Northern Regional Fisheries Board
Station Road
Ballyshannon
Co. Donegal
Tel (072) 51435

Irish Specimen Fish Committee
Balnagowan House
Mobhi Boreen
Glasnevin
Dublin 9
Tel (01) 379206

National Coarse Fishing Federation of Ireland
Mr Brendan Coulter
Hon. Sec.
'Blaithin'
Dublin Road
Cavan
Tel (049) 32367

Federation of Pike Angler Clubs
Mr John Chambers
Templeogue Village
Dublin 6
Tel (01) 904454

Bord Failte
Baggot Street Bridge
Dublin 2
Tel (01) 765871

Paul Harris, Irish Tourist Board Angling Representative
47 The Crescent
Brinklow, Nr Rugby
Warwickshire, CU23 OLG
England
Tel (0786) 833203

COARSE AND PIKE FISHING BYE LAWS IN IRELAND

1. It is illegal to have or to use live fish as bait.
2. The only legal method to catch freshwater fish is by rod and line.
3. A person may fish with not more than two rods at any time.
4. It is illegal to transfer live Roach from one water to any other waters. Offenders may be prosecuted.

Bye Law No. 667 relates to Pike. It prohibits:

(a) the taking or killing by any person of more than one Pike on any day;

(b) the taking or killing by any person of any Pike exceeding 6.6 lbs (3 kg) in weight;

(c) any person having in his possession more than one dead whole Pike or alternatively, more than 3.3 lbs (1.5 kg) by weight of Pike flesh or parts.

(d) An exception to the above – One whole and ungutted Pike of *specimen* size may be taken. River specimen Pike – 20 lbs (9.072 kg); Lake specimen Pike – 30 lbs (13.608 kg).

Note: Penalties for breach of the above laws include confiscation of tackle and heavy fines.

SPECIMEN AND RECORD FISH

The Irish Specimen Fish Committee consists of representatives of the various Irish Angling Federations, government departments and official organisations with an interest in Irish angling. Its objective is to verify, record and publicise the capture on rod and line of Record and 'Specimen' fish in Irish waters. A list of specimen fish is published annually and is available from Hon. Secretary, Irish Specimen Fish Committee at the Central Fisheries Board, Glasnevin, Dublin 9. Only fish which can be fully vouched for as to weight and species can be accepted. Specimen awards are presented annually, usually at functions in Dublin and Belfast. Claim forms are available from the Hon. Secretary, or from local clubs and tackle shops. The following is a schedule of Record and Specimen Weights.

IRISH RECORD FISH

FRESHWATER SPECIES

SPECIES	WEIGHT LBS OZ	DATE OF CAPTURE	PLACE OF CAPTURE	CAPTOR
Salmon	57 0	1874	River Suir	M. Maher
Sea Trout	16 6	29.10.1983	Shimna River, Co. Down	Thomas McManus
Brown Trout (River)	20 0	22.2.1957	River Shannon, Corbally	Major Hugh Place
Brown Trout (Lake)	26 2	15.7.1894	Lough Ennel	Wm. Mears
Bream	11 12	1882	River Blackwater (Monaghan)	A. Pike
Carp	26 2	28.5.1989	The Lough, Cork	Kieron V. Bend
Dace	1 2	8.8.1966	River Blackwater Cappoquin	John T. Henry
Perch	5 8	1946	Lough Erne	S. Drum
Pike (River)	42 0	22.3.1964	River Barrow	M. Watkins
Pike (Lake)	38 2	25.2.1973	Lough Corrib	Brendan Hardiman
Roach	2 13½	11.8.1970	River Blackwater, Cappoquin	Lawrie Robinson
Rudd	3 4	27.5.1991	Annaghmore Lough	Steve Wilks
Rudd/Bream Hybrid	6 4	5.3.1990	Monalty Lake	Peter Walsh
Roach/Bream Hybrid	2.06 kg	2.7.1989	Drumreask L.	Philip Arthur
Tench	7 13¼	25.5.1971	River Shannon, Lanesboro	Raymond Webb
River Eel	6 15	12.6.1979	L. Droumenisa, Bantry	J. Murnane

MARINE SPECIES

SPECIES	WEIGHT LBS OZ	DATE OF CAPTURE	PLACE OF CAPTURE	CAPTOR
Angler Fish	42.985 kg	3.11.1985	Belfast Lough	Sean Neill
Bass	17 1¼	27.4.1977	Whiting Bay, Ardmore	Malcolm Tucker
Black Sole	6.32 lbs	28.12.1986	Ballycotton	Eddie Cull
Brill	9 8	8.9.1984	Causeway Coast	Deborah Gregg
Coalfish	12.5 kg	21.9.1983	Kinsale	E. Masheijer
Cod	42 0	1921	Ballycotton	I. L. Stewart
Conger	72 0	June 1914	Valentia	J. Green
Dab	2.02	28.1.1989	Dunmore East	Paul Beglin
Spur Dogfish	18 12	10.9.1977	Bantry	John Murnane
Greater Spotted Dogfish	23 12	29.5.1983	Valentia	Tony Outmayjer

SPECIES	WEIGHT LBS OZ	DATE OF CAPTURE	PLACE OF CAPTURE	CAPTOR
Lesser Spotted Dogfish	4 4	26.7.1982	Valentia	Cor Heinis
Flounder	4.60	9.11.1991	Ballyteigue, Co. Wexford	Patrick Cassidy
Garfish	3 10¼	16.9.1967	Kinsale	Even Bazard
Tub Gurnard	12 3½	8.8.1973	Bullsmouth, Achill	Robert Seaman
Grey Gurnard	3 1	21.9.1967	Rosslare Bay	Brendan Walsh
Red Gurnard	3 9½	17.7.1968	Belmullet	James Prescott
Haddock	10 13½	15.7.1964	Kinsale	F.A.E. Bull
Hake	25 5½	28.4.1962	Belfast Lough	H.W. Steele
Halibut	156	23.7.1972	Belmullet	Frank Brogan
Herring .	425 kg	11.7.1986	Rathlin Island	Wm. McMath
John Dory	7 8	12.8.1984	Killala Bay	Cleona Walkin
Ling	46 8	26.7.1965	Kinsale	A.J.C. Bull
Mackerel	4 2	18.9.1979	Ballycotton	Ulrich Plassmann
Megrim	1.85 kg	26.7.1987	Killala	Paul Hennigan
Monkfish	73 0	1.6.1980	Fenit	James Boyd
Grey Mullet	7 10	8.6.1972	Killybegs Pier	Kevin Boyle
Plaice	8.23	23.1.1982	Ballycotton Pier	Edmund Cull
Pollack	19 3	1904	Ballycotton	J.N. Hearne
Pouting	4 13½	2.4.1983	Kilmore Quay	John Devereaux
Thornback Ray	37 0	28.5.1961	Ling Rocks, Kinsale	M.J. Fitzgerald
Blonde Ray	36 8	9.9.1964	Cork Harbour	D. Minchin
Sting Ray	51 0	8.8.1970	Fenit	John White
Cuckoo Ray	5 11	3.8.1975	Causeway Coast	V. Morrison
Undulate Ray	18	11.6.1977	Fenit	Ann-Mari Liedecke
Homelyn Ray	8.28	28.9.1983	Cork Harbour	Edmund Cull
Painted Ray	14.37	18.6.1980	Garryvoe	Edmund Cull
Electric Ray	69	5.9.1977	Courtmacsherry	J. Rynsburger
Ray's Bream	6 4¼	26.8.1979	Valentia	Martin Sarney
Red Sea Bream	9 6	24.8.1963	Valentia	P. Maguire
Twaite Shad	2.87	5.5.1985	St Mullins	Peter McCartin
Porbeagle Shark	365	1932	Keem Bay, Achill	Dr O'Donel Brown
Blue Shark	206	7.10.1959	Achill Head	J. McMonagle
Six Gilled Shark	154	28.8.1968	Kinsale	Andrew Bull
Common Skate	221	1913	Ballycotton	T. Tucker
White Skate	165	7.8.1966	Clew Bay	Jack Stack
Scad	1.97 lbs	6.9.1986	Clonakilty	Master R. McCarthy
Smooth Hound	13.75	27.6.1991	Five Mile Pt.	Peter Mooney
Stone Basse	10 13	2.8.1989	Kinsale	Stefano D'Amico

Three Bearded Rockling	3	1	11.5.90	Arklow	Maurice Laurent
Tope	66	8	15.7.1979	Carlingford Lough	Cyril Young
Torsk	4.7 kg		20.5.1989	Burtonport	Colin Hutton
Turbot	34		9.6.1982	Cork Harbour	Frank Fleming
Whiting	4	14½	19.3.1981	Kenmare Bay	Comdt. M.J. O'Connor
Ballan Wrasse	4.3 kg		20.8.1983	Clogher Head	Bertrand Kron
Cuckoo Wrasse	1.94		24.8.1991	Carne	Cecil Barron

SCHEDULE OF SPECIMEN WEIGHTS (REVISED)

FRESHWATER FISH	IRISH RECORD		SPECIMEN WEIGHT	
	LBS	OZ	LBS	KG
Salmon *(Salmo salar)*	57	0	20	9.072
Sea Trout *(Salmo trutta)*	16	6	6	2.721
Brown Trout *(Salmo trutta) (River)*	20	0	5	2.268
Brown Trout *(Salmo trutta) (Lake)*	26	2	10	4.536
Slob Trout *(Salmo trutta)*	–	–	10	4.536
Bream *(Abramis brama)*	11	12	7½	3.402
Carp *(Cyprinus carpio)*	26	2	10	4.536
Dace *(Leuciscus leuciscus)*	1	2	1	.454
Perch *(Perca fluviatilis)*	5	8	3	1.361
Pike *(Esox lucius) (Lake)*	38	2	30	13.608
Pike *(Esox lucius) (River)*	42	0	20	9.072
Roach *(Rutilus rutilus)*	2	13½	2	.907
Rudd *(Scardinius erythrophthalmus)*	3	1	2¼	1.021
Rudd/Bream hybrid	6	4	3	1.361
Roach/Bream hybrid	2.065 kg		3	1.361
Tench *(Tinca tinca)*	7	13¼	6	2.721
Eel *(Anguilla anguilla)*	6	15	3	1.361

SEA FISH	IRISH RECORD		SPECIMEN WEIGHT	
	LBS	OZ	LBS	KG
Angler fish *(Lophius piscatorius)*	42.985 kg		40	18.144
Bass *(Dicentrarchus labrax)*	17	1¼	10	4.536
Black Sole *(Solea solea)*	6.32		2	.907
Brill *(Scophthalmus rhombus)*	9	8	5	2.268
Coalfish *(Pollachius virens)*	12.5 kg		15	6.804
Cod *(Gadus morhua)*	42	0	25	11.340
Conger *(Conger conger)*	72	0	40	18.144
Dab *(Limanda limanda)*	2.02		1½	.680
Dogfish				
– Spur *(Squalus acanthias)*	18	12	12	5.443
– Lesser Spotted *(Scyliorhinus caniculus)*	4	4	3½	1.587
– Greater Spotted *(Scyliorhinus stellaris)*	23	12	16	7.257

SEA FISH		IRISH RECORD		SPECIMEN WEIGHT	
		LBS	OZ	LBS	KG
Flounder *(Platichthys flesus)*		4.60		3	1.361
Garfish *(Belone belone)*		3	10¼	2¼	1.021
(Belone svetovidovi)		1	0	14 ozs	.355
Gurnard	– Tub *(Trigla lucerna)*	12	3½	5	2.268
	– Grey *(Eutrigla gurnardus)*	3	1	1½	.680
	– Red *(Aspitigla cuculus)*	3	9½	2	.907
Haddock *(Melanogrammus aeglifinus)*		10	13½	7	3.175
Hake *(Merluccius merluccius)*		25	5½	10	4.536
Halibut *(Hippoglossus hippoglossus)*		156	0	50	22.680
Herring *(Culpea harengus)*		.425 kg		¾	.340
John Dory *(Zeus faber)*		7	8	4	1.814
Ling *(Molva molva)*		46	8	25	11.340
Mackerel *(Scomber scombrus)*		4	2	2½	1.134
Megrim *(Lepidorhombus whiffiagonis)*		1.85 kg		1¾	.794
Monkfish *(Squatina squatina)*		73	0	50	22.680
Mullet	– Grey, thick lipped *(Crenimugil labrosus)*	7	10	5	2.268
	– Red *(Mullus surmuletus)*	–	–	1	.454
Plaice *(Pleuronectes platessa)*		8.23		4	1.814
Pollack *(Pollachius pollachius)*		19	3	12	5.443
Pouting *(Trisopterus luscus)*		4	13½	3	1.361
Ray	– Thornback *(Raja clavata)*	37	0	20	9.072
	– Blonde *(Raja brachyura)*	36	8	25	11.340
	– Cuckoo *(Raja naevus)*	5	11	4½	2.041
	– Electric *(Torpedo nobiliana)*	69	0	20	9.072
	– Homelyn *(Raja montagui)*	8.28		5	2.268
	– Undulate *(Raja undulata)*	18		14	6.350
	– Painted *(Raja microocellata)*	14.37		10	4.536
	– Sting *(Dasyatis pastinaca)*	51		30	13.608
Ray's Bream *(Brama brama)*		6	4¼	5	2.268
Red Sea Bream *(Pagellus bogaraveo)*		9	6	4½	2.041
Rockling, Three Bearded *(Gaidropsarus vulgaris)*		3	1	1¾	.794
Scad *(Trachurus trachurus)*		1.97		1½	.680
Shad	– Allis *(Alosa alosa)*	–		4	1.814
	– Twaite *(Alosa fallax)*	2.87		2	.907
Shark	– Porbeagle *(Lamna nasus)*	365	0	150	68.038
	– Blue *(Prionace glauca)*	206	0	100	45.359
	– Thresher *(Alopias vulpinus)*	–	–	120	54.431
	– Mako *(Isurus oxyrinchus)*	–	–	200	90.718
	– Six-Gilled *(Hexanchus griseus)*	154		100	45.359

Skate – Common *(Raja batis)*	221	0		suspended
– White *(Raja alba)*	165	0	120	54.431
– Long Nose *(Raja oxyrinchus)*	–	–	80	36.287
Smooth Hound *(Mustelus asterias)*	13.75		7	3.175
Stone Basse *(Polyprion americanus)*	10	13	8	3.628
Tope *(Galeorhinus galeus)*	66	8	40	18.144
Torsk *(Brosme brosme)*	4.7 kg		6	2.721
Trigger Fish *(Balistes carolinensis)*			3.25	1.474
Tunny *(Thunnus thynnus)*	–	–	100	45.359
Turbot *(Scophthalmus maximus)*	34	0	18	8.165
Whiting *(Merlangus merlangus)*	4	14½	3	1.361
Wrasse, Ballan *(Labrus bergylta)*	4.3 kg		4¾	2.154
Wrasse, Cuckoo *(Labrus mixtus)*	1.94		1¼	.567

Angling for the More Common Species in Ireland

■ BREAM *(Abramis brama)*

IRISH RECORD: 11 lbs 12 oz in River Blackwater, Co. Monaghan in 1882.
SPECIMEN WEIGHT: 7½ lbs.

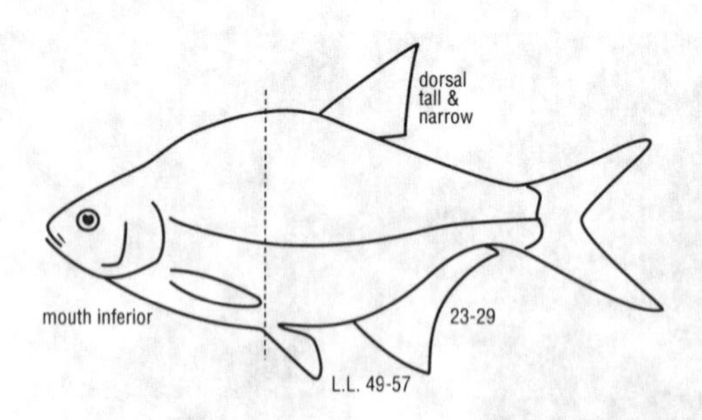

Ir. Bran; Fr. Brême; Ge. Blei, Brachsen; Du. Brasom; It. Brama.
Mouth inferior. Dorsal short-based, but high and 'peaked', its origin some distance behind insertion of pelvic fins. Anal fin very long, with 23–29 branched rays. Tail-fin large, deeply forked, the lower lobe the longer. 49–57 scales along the lateral line. Very slimy. Young fish (up to about 12 inches) greyish above, silvery on the sides, fins grey. Large fish bronze, with very dark fins. Grows to over 12 lbs.

Ireland is renowned for its wild and well-conditioned Bream and the very special sport that they offer the angler. To say it offers the best all-round package in Europe is not an idle boast. You will find Bream widely spread in Ireland's limestone fisheries, but the sluggish waters within the catchment areas of the River Erne and River Shannon are outstanding.

Bream angling is generally at its best from later April to October, with some exceptions where the fish need high water temperatures and settled summer levels to really come on the feed. You should take note that Bream spawn from about mid-May to late June when they shoal up in shallow water.

The Bream is a shoal fish, and shoals move considerable distances. You have to hold them in your swim. As some Irish waters, even some big and well-known ones, seldom see an angler, this will require considerable baiting and patience. Don't spare the ground bait. If results are disappointing, do not move on to another water. Stay with your baited swim. You will be pleasantly surprised when those Bream find your groundbait.

Red worms and brandlings, with maggot or caster, are the most successful baits. Bread and sweetcorn are also used with success.

Quality Bream frequent Irish canals as well as rivers and lakes. In the Guide, we list most of those Bream waters which are accessible. Just select any of the listed areas, enquire from your accommodation host and you cannot go wrong.

■ RUDD *(Scardinius erythrophthalmus)*

IRISH RECORD: 3 lbs 4 oz, Annaghmore Lake, Strokestown, 1991.

SPECIMEN WEIGHT: 2¼ lbs.

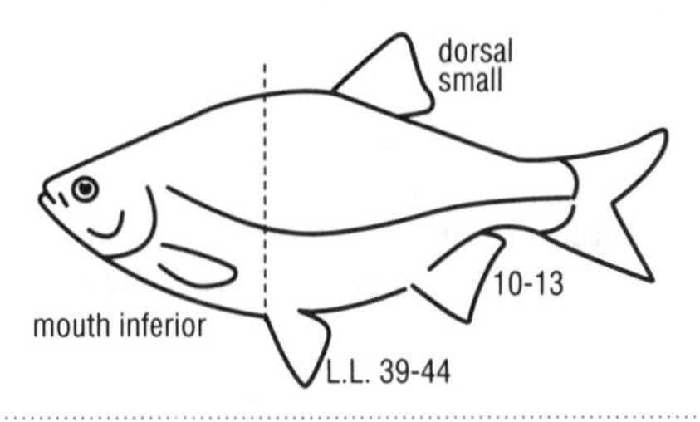

Ir. Ruán; Fr. Rotengle; Ge. Rotfeder; Du. Ruisvoorn; It. Scardola.

Cleft of mouth directed obliquely upwards; dorsal fin small, its origin well behind insertion of pelvic fins. Anal fin short, with 10–13 branched rays. 39–44 scales along lateral line. Young blue and silver; large fish green-backed, with a golden lustre on the sides. Dorsal reddish-brown; pelvics, anal and tail-fin red. Grows to about 4 lb. Commonly miscalled 'Roach'.

Rudd are shy fish, so it is essential to fish quietly and not disturb the shoal. They are mid-water and surface feeders, preferring the weedy, reedy areas of lakes, rivers and canals. They are most active in warm conditions and a cold day will often put them off the feed.

Maggots are the most successful bait and bread flake will take the bigger fish.

Rudd inhabit a great number of waters throughout Ireland and spawn between May and July. They are beautifully coloured fish, often confused with Roach.

Part of the enjoyment of Ireland is the adventure and enjoyment derived from exploring and finding new waters that can offer quality sport. Few countries can offer such an opportunity and anyone who explores the quiet, seldom-used waters will be generously rewarded.

■ TENCH *(Tinca tinca)*

IRISH RECORD: 7 lbs 13.25 oz in the River Shannon at Lanesborough, 1971.
SPECIMEN WEIGHT: 6 lbs.

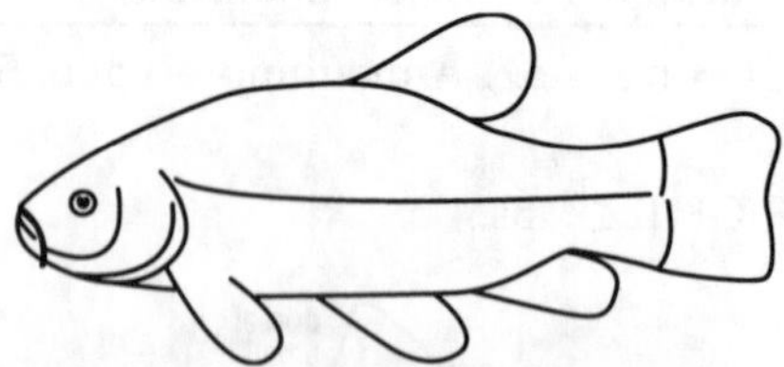

Ir. Cúramán; Fr. Tanche; Ge. Schleie; Du. Zeelt; It. Tinca; Sp. Tenca.
A thick-set fish with strong fins. Dorsal short, rounded, tail-fin only slightly concave. Pelvic fins very large, spoon shaped and with greatly thickened anterior rays in adult males. A pair of minute barbels attached to mouth. Greenish olive, with orange-red eyes. Grows to about 10 lbs.

Look for weedy, still waters with muddy bottoms. Above all else, look for tell-tale bubbles on the water surfaces. They spell out the underwater activity, the commotion being caused by bottom-feeding fish as they disturb the bottom. They will be Tench!

Prepare your swim well. It may be necessary to rake it and then feed with the bait of your choice. Fishing is by float or leger. When hooked, they will make for the weeds, so don't use light tackle for Irish Tench.

Ireland's canals as well as its many lakes and some river stretches offer good Tench fishing. Lake and river fishing do not get under way properly until May to June. It tends to deteriorate in the high summer and comes back again in September. The canals, on the other hand, can offer excellent sport from late April going right through into October. Tench fishing is best in most waters in the early morning and late evening.

■ ROACH *(Rutilus rutilus)*

IRISH RECORD: 2 lbs 13.5 oz in the River Blackwater at Cappoquin.
SPECIMEN WEIGHT: 2 lbs.

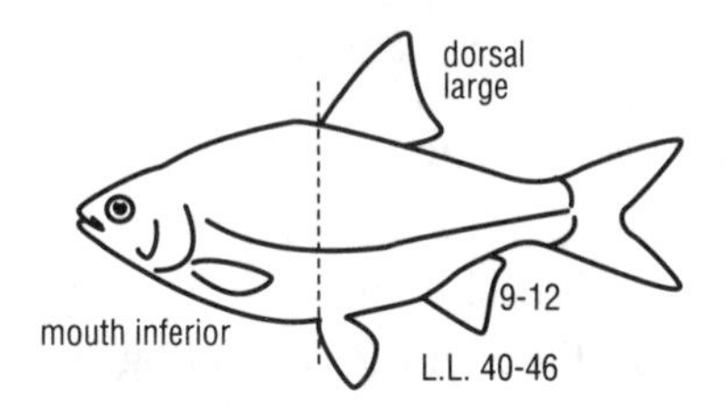

Ir. Róiste; Fr. Gardon; Ge. Plötz, Rotauge; Du. Blankvoorn; It. Triotto; Sp. Bermejulea. Mouth inferior; dorsal fin noticeably large, with its origin over the insertion of the pelvic fins. Anal fin short, with 9–12 branched rays (excluding the unbranched ray at the leading edge of the fin and the short rays fused with it). 40–46 scales along lateral line. Blue on the back, silvery on the sides (sometimes with a bronze lustre in big fish); dorsal, brownish red; pelvics, anal and tail-fin red. Grows to about 4 lbs. Now spreading through most major river systems.

Roach are not indigenous to Ireland. They were first introduced to the Munster River Blackwater at the end of the 19th century and are now pretty widespread. Roach are prolific and are appearing in new waters on a regular basis.

Roach spawn mostly in weed in still or moving water from May into June. They will move considerable distances to find suitable spawning ground. In many cases they will leave lakes, moving into rivers to spawn.

Maggots or caster are the popular baits. They are mid water to bottom feeders and can be taken by float or leger fishing.

■ PIKE *(Esox lucius)*

IRISH RECORD FOR RIVER: 42 lbs on the River Barrow south of Carlow, 1964.
IRISH RECORD FOR LAKE: 28 lbs 2 oz.
SPECIMEN WEIGHTS: River – 20 lbs; Lake – 30 lbs.

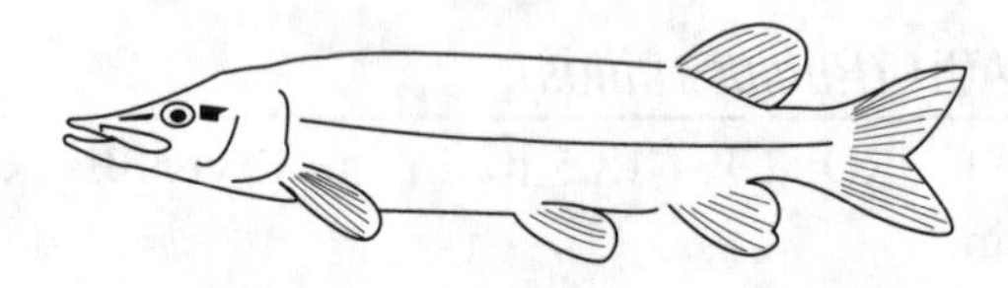

Ir. Liús; Fr. Brochet; Ge. Hecht; Du Snoek; It. Luccio; Sp. Lucio.
Torpedo-shaped body; shovel-like snout; large mouth with many sharp teeth; single dorsal fin set far back, over the anal fin. Greenish olive, mottled with lighter patches; the young have a more barred coloration. Grows to about 60 lb.

Stories about mammoth Irish Pike are legendary. In any of the authoritative texts on Pike and Pike angling, Ireland is given pride of place.

Irish Pike grow faster than most other species. They fight better when at the business end of the tackle and they are exceptionally healthy and well conditioned. The stability of environment, particularly of the large Irish lakes, is most often given as the cause factor.

Pike fisheries are widespread in Ireland. Look for waters where there is a generous supply of weed growth and which hold a large stock of fodder fish such as Roach, Rudd, Perch and Bream. The big Irish lakes and big rivers will oblige.

Different angling methods are successful throughout the season. In the summer, the best Pike angling results come from spinning artificial baits such as spoons, plugs etc. At that time of the year, Pike often remain close to the weedy margins, making occasional dashes to feed on the unsuspecting small fish.

In the autumn and through the winter, legering with dead Rudd or Roach will get good results. From the first cold days, legering with Herring, Mackerel, Smelt or other baits is most successful. Casting a small dead fish using the 'sink and draw' method is effective and trolling a bait from a moving boat will also be rewarding.

Pike generally spawn in shallow, grassy margins from mid February to April.

PIKE CONSERVATION

- Anglers are encouraged to conserve stocks of Pike. Local Pike clubs in Ireland return all Pike alive to the water and we urge all others to do likewise.
- It is essential when Pike fishing to do so with special attention to the care of the fish, in landing and removing the hook or hooks.
- First, use small hooks, which are barbless or semi-barbed. Strike quickly on a tight line. Never leave a rod unattended.
- Always use a net to land the Pike. Never use a gaff. Put the Pike on soft ground or, if in a boat, use a piece of old carpet as a mat. With the fish on its back, insert two fingers inside the gill cover and between it and the outside gill raker. Then lift the head. The mouth will open, and by using long straight forceps, you can remove the hook.
- Weigh the fish in a sling. Never insert the scales hook into the Pike. Return the Pike carefully to the water. If it rolls on its side, hold it or lock it gently between two banksticks until it recovers from its ordeal on the bank. The Pike will soon move off into deep water.

SPECIAL NOTICE

PIKE

1. It is illegal to have or to use live fish as bait.
2. The only legal method to catch freshwater fish is by rod and line.
3. A person may fish with not more than two rods at any time.
4. It is illegal to transfer live Roach from one water to any other waters. Offenders may be prosecuted.

BYE LAW NO. 667 PROHIBITS:

(a) the taking or killing by any person of more than one Pike on any day;

(b) the taking or killing by any person of any Pike exceeding 6.6 lbs (3 kg) in weight;

(c) any person having in his possession more than one dead whole Pike or alternatively, more than 3.3 lbs (1.5 kg) by weight of Pike flesh or parts.

(d) An exception to the above – One whole and ungutted Pike of *specimen* size may be taken. River specimen Pike – 20 lbs (9.072 kg); Lake specimen Pike – 30 lbs (13.608 kg).

Note: Penalties for breach of the above laws include confiscation of tackle and heavy fines.

PERCH *(Perca fluviatilis)*

IRISH RECORD: 5 lbs 8 oz in Lough Erne, 1956.
SPECIMEN WEIGHT: 3 lbs.

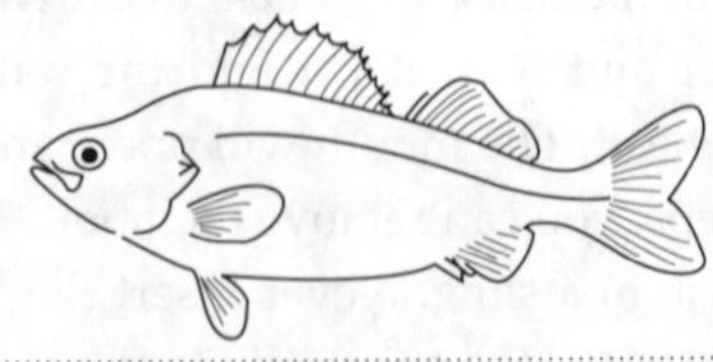

Ir. Péirse; Fr. Perche; Ge. Baarsch; Du. Baars; It. Pesce Persico; Sp. Perca.

Two dorsal fins set close together, the first with sharp spines. Spines also in the origin of the anal fin and in the origin of the pelvic fins, which are placed under the pectorals. Greenish-olive, with black bars on the sides; pelvics, anal and tail-fin red or orange. Grows to about 6 lb.

Really big Perch are a rarity in Irish waters but that is the only negative thing about them. They are found almost everywhere, including game fisheries, and will respond to a legion of angling bait. Perch are predators and will take spinning bait, but the maggot and common worm will also bring success.

Perch spawn from mid April into mid May. During the warm summer months, it is common to see shoals of small Perch in the shallow margins.

DACE *(Leuciscus leuciscus)*

IRISH RECORD: 1 lb 2 oz River Blackwater, 1966.
SPECIMEN WEIGHT: 1 lb.

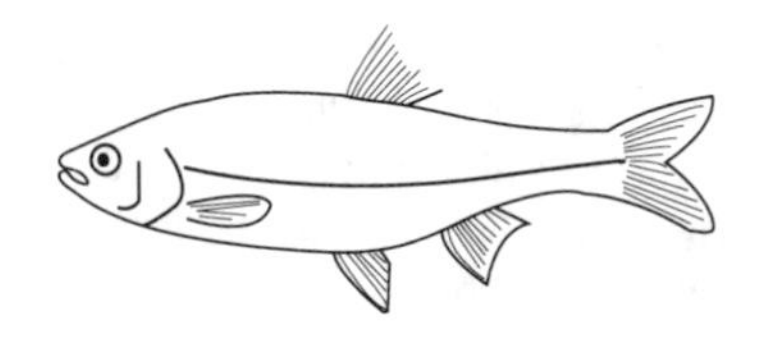

Ir. Déas; Fr. Vandois; Ge. Hasel; Du. Serpeling.
More slender than Roach or Rudd (which see). Olive on the back, silvery on the sides; pelvics, anal and tail-fin pinkish-brown or sepia. From the Chub (which does not occur in Ireland) the Dace is distinguished by its smaller head and concave dorsal and anal fins (convex in the Chub). Grows to about 1½ lbs. In Ireland, found only in the Cork Blackwater system and one lake in Co. Clare.

Dace are to be found in the Munster (Cork) Blackwater. They provide great sport to those fishing light tackle. Dace live in shoals and move close to the surface in streamy sections of the river. Their favourite haunts are near weirs. In the colder months, they will be found in quieter water and deep holes.

Dace are fished for with light tackle. They will respond to maggots or bread flake on float tackle. They spawn from April to May.

CARP *(Cyprinus carpio)*

IRISH RECORD: 26 lbs 2 oz, the Lough, Cork City, 1989.
SPECIMEN WEIGHT: 10 lbs.

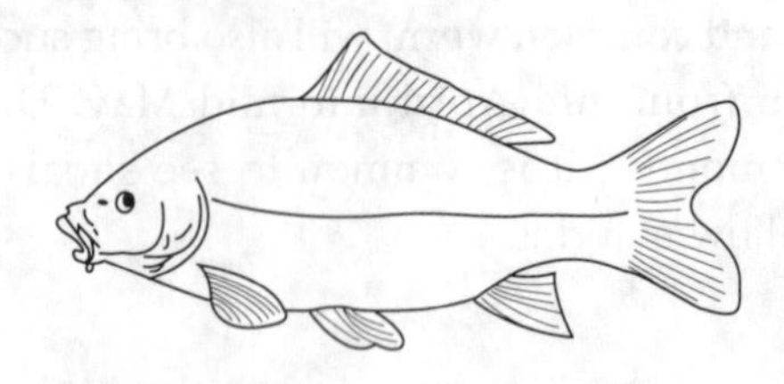

Ir. Carbán; Fr. Carpé; Ge. Karpfen; Du. Karper; It. Carpa; Sp. Carpa.
Mouth inferior, with thick lips and two pairs of barbels, one pair long. Tail-fin forked; dorsal fin long; a barbed, bony ray in the origin of the dorsal and in the origin of the anal fin. Several varieties, differing considerably in scaling and height of body, including (a) fully-scaled Carp, some long-bodied ('wild Carp'), others deep bodied ('fully-scaled King Carp'); (b) mirror Carp, with some greatly enlarged and shining scales (sometimes in rows, sometimes haphazardly distributed) on otherwise naked bodies; (c) leather Carp, with a thick skin and only a few scales or none; (d) a leaden-coloured form, which appears naked, but really has a full covering of very thin scales entirely devoid of pigment. Carp grow to over 40 lb. Localised.

Carp are to be found in few waters in Ireland. The best fishery is The Lough in Cork City which has a good stock of Carp increasing in weight annually. Carp are fished for by float or leger and will respond to a great number of baits. Sweetcorn, maggot, bread are common but now, boilies and other manufactured baits are used. Strong tackle is necessary as Carp are strong and powerful fighters.

COUNTIES OF IRELAND

County Carlow

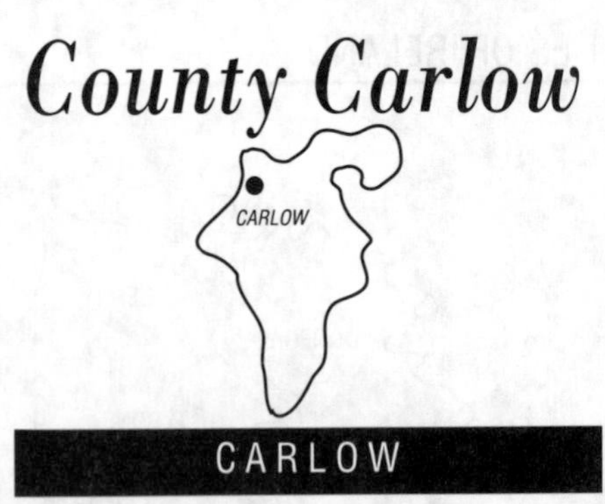

CARLOW

Carlow is on the River Barrow and is situated on the Dublin-Kilkenny road (N9) about 45 miles (70 km) south-west of Dublin. It is a busy town with all modern facilities. The wide river flows through here, and the town along the western bank is called Graiguecullen. Bream fishing is good from late April to October and Rudd feed freely in the summer months. Pike fishing is good all year, but the best results come in the colder months. Tench fishing is best in May and June. Fishing in this area is in the River Barrow.

CLUBS

Carlow and Graiguecullen Angling Club, Joe Nolan, St Fiach's Terrace, Graiguecullen.
Leighlinbridge Anglers Club, Elaine Meaney, Meaney's Pub, Leighlinbridge, Tel (0503) 21321.

ANGLING CONTACTS

Guesthouse owners are experienced in dealing with anglers.
Irwin Hutchinson, Chairman, Carlow CAC, Beechwood Park, Pollerton, Co. Carlow, Tel (0503) 32592.
John Butler, Castle Hill, Graiguecullen, Tel (0503) 41647.
Tom Dermody, Leighlinbridge.

TACKLE SHOPS

John Boyd, Motor and Sports, Castle Arcade, Castle Street, Carlow.
Griffin Hawe Ltd, 22 Duke Street, Athy, Tel (0507) 31221.

BAIT

John Boyd, Motor and Sports, Castle Arcade, Castle Street, Carlow.

Griffin Hawe Ltd, 22 Duke Street, Athy, Tel (0507) 31221.

CARLOW

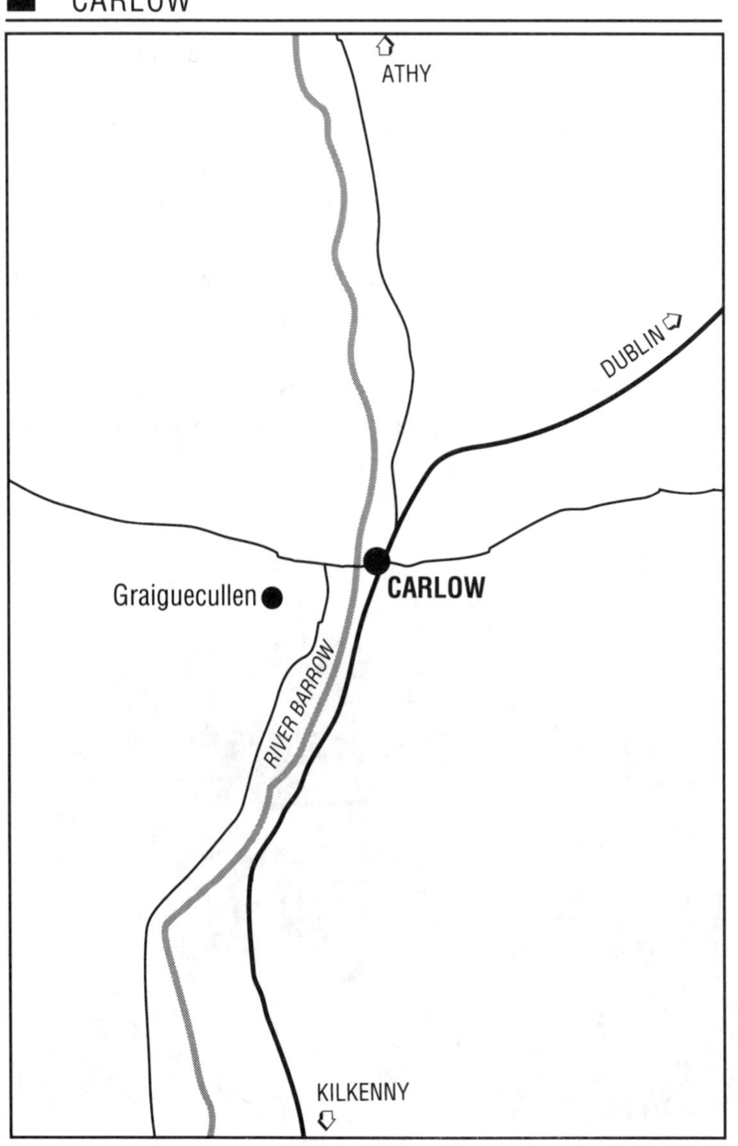

OTHER WATERS IN THIS AREA

See Athy, Graiguenamanagh, Vicarstown.

SPECIES

Bream, Rudd, Hybrids, Perch, Pike, Eels, some Tench.

RIVER BARROW: The river above Carlow along the east bank at the bacon factory stretch produces good Bream and Rudd in the summer months.

Catches over 100 lbs (45 kg) are taken in the stretch below the town, where Bream are to 5 lbs (2.2 kg) and Rudd to 2 lbs (0.9 kg). The short stretch behind the island below Graiguecullen is good for Rudd and Tench in May/June. Downriver from Milford, the river to Leighlinbridge and below the town holds stocks of good Rudd and Pike with Bream and Eels.

Special Note: The River Barrow is a mixed fishery with Salmon and Trout. Anglers should note the game fishing stretches and observe all local club regulations.

County Cavan

ARVA

Arva is a small town in Co. Cavan near the Leitrim and Longford borders near Gowna and Carrigallen. Bream and Roach fishing are good from late April to October, with Roach in some waters continuing throughout the year. Pike, which can be taken all year, are at their best in the winter months. Fishing in this area is mostly in lakes.

CLUB

Arva Tourism Association, Pat Doyle, Hollybank House, Arva, Tel (049) 35254.

ANGLING CONTACT

Guesthouse owners in this area are experienced in dealing with anglers.

TACKLE SHOPS

O'Connors, General Shop, Main Street.
Smith's General Shop, Main Street.

BAIT

Eamonn Grey, Breffni Arms, Main Street, Arva, Tel (049) 35127.

OTHER WATERS IN THIS AREA

See Gowna, Carrigallen, Killeshandra, Cavan.

MAPS

Central Fisheries Board Angling Maps – Arva-Killeshandra, Gowna-Arva, Cavan.

COMPETITIONS

Arva Festival, early September.

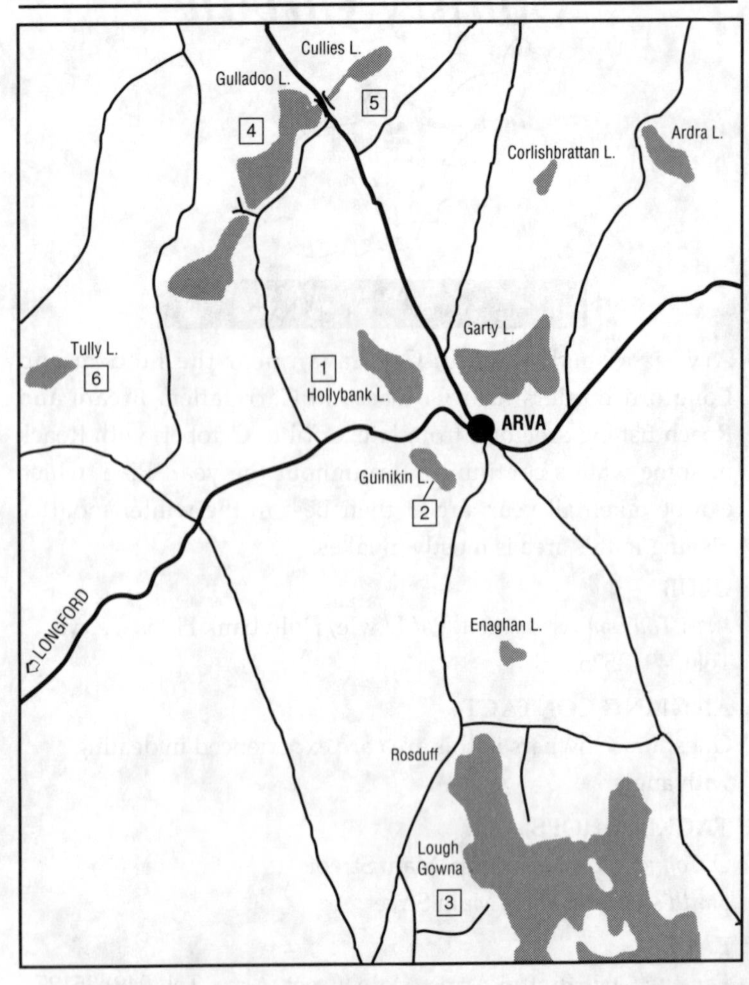

1. HOLLYBANK LAKE: A first class fishery for Roach, small Bream and Hybrids. It also holds Perch, Pike and Eels. Access is off the Carrigallen road.
2. GUINIKEN LAKE: This lake, just 1 mile (1.6 km) from the town, is good for Tench to 4 lbs (1.8 kg) in May/June. The water also has Roach, Perch, Pike and Eels.
3. STRETTON'S SHORE, LOUGH GOWNA: In the western part of Lough Gowna, this is a good stretch with very good

Bream fishing into deep water. It also holds Roach, Hybrids, Perch, Pike and Eels. The shore opposite, at Rosduff, is also fishable and produces good results. This is a good match stretch for 50 anglers.

4. GULLADOO LAKE: The upper lake, above the bridge and to the right, has a short stretch which is good for Bream and Roach. The best Bream in the lower lake is at the narrow part, where great catches of Roach and Hybrids are taken. This lake also holds good stocks of Perch, Pike and Eels.
5. CULLIES LAKE: To the right, off the Carrigallen road, this lake to the left is also good for Bream to 4 lbs (1.8 kg), with a big stock of Perch, Roach, Pike and Eels.
6. TULLY LAKE: Off the Carrigallen Road and through Moyne, this is a good water producing great Bream catches with fish to 4 lbs (1.8 kg). It also has Roach, Hybrids, Perch, Pike and Eels.

BAILIEBOROUGH

Bailieborough, situated on high ground, is on the Cavan-Kingscourt road (R165). This is an industrious town in east Co. Cavan. It is at the top of one arm of the Boyne system where there are good fishing lakes. Bream fishing is good from April to October, with Roach and Pike fishing throughout the year in this area, where fishing is in lakes.

CLUB

Bailieborough Tourist Development Association, Mrs B. Halloran, Droimlinn, Bailieborough, Tel (042) 62520.

ANGLING CONTACTS

Guesthouse owners in this area are experienced in dealing with anglers.

TACKLE SHOPS

McElwaines, Main Street, Bailieborough, Tel (042) 65341.

BAIT

McElwaines, Main Street.

OTHER WATERS IN THIS AREA

See Virginia, Shercock, Kingscourt, Cootehill.

SPECIES

Bream, Roach, Hybrids, Perch, Pike, Eels.

MAPS

Central and Regional Fisheries Board Angling Maps – Bailieborough/Virginia, Cootehill/Shercock, Carrickmacross/Drumconrath.

BAILIEBOROUGH

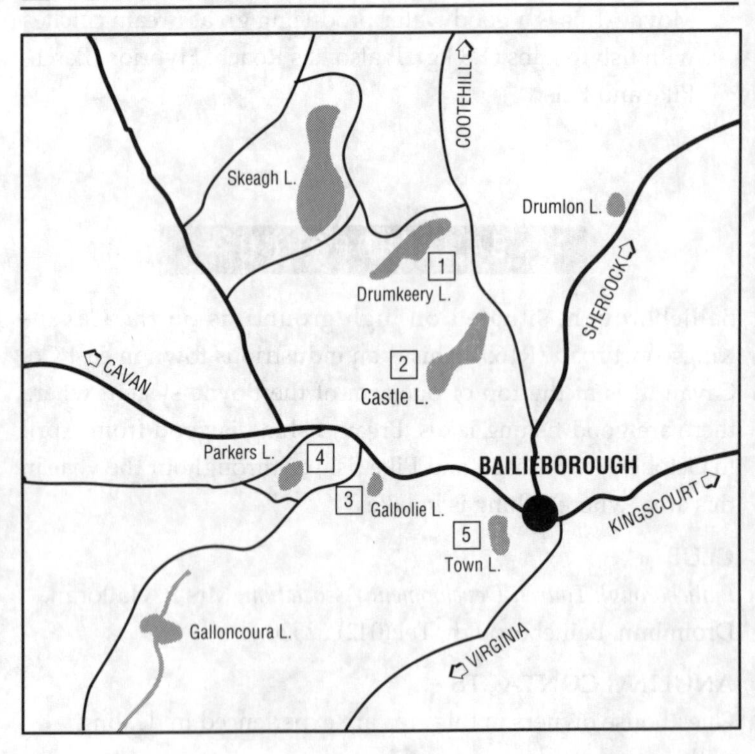

1. DRUMKEERY LAKE: This 40-acre lake is 3 miles (5 km) from the town. Access is easy to the lake, which has a firm shore. This good water holds Bream to 4 lbs (1.8 kg), Roach, Hybrids, Perch, Pike and Eels.
2. CASTLE LAKE: This is a 50 acre lake, located in a forest. Parking and access are good. It is a rich fishery which provides good sport for Bream, Roach, Hybrids, Perch, Pike and Eels. Please respect Forestry regulations. Leave no litter and do not light fires.
3. GALBOLIE LAKE: This is a small lake beside the Cavan road. Fishing is from stands for some Bream, Roach, Perch, Pike and Eels.
4. PARKERS LAKE: This 15 acre lake is 3 miles (5 km) from the town. The water is reeded and holds a good stock of quality Bream, with Roach, Perch, Pike and Eels. Access is over private ground. Stiles, fishing stands and foot bridges are provided.
5. TOWN LAKE: Situated west of the town, this fishery of 20 acres provides good sport for Roach, Bream, Perch, Pike and Eels. Access is easy and there is some bank fishing, while at other places there are stands.

BALLYCONNELL

Ballyconnell is situated on the Cavan-Swanlinbar road. It's a small, tidy town which has the Woodford River/Canal flowing through it. Roach and Pike fishing continues throughout the year, but the best results come in the winter months. Bream fishing is from mid April to October. Tench fishing is best in May/June.

CLUB

Ballyconnell Tourist and Angling Association, Fidelma Rea, Main Street, Ballyconnell.

ANGLING CONTACTS

Francis McGoldrick, Anglers Rest, Ballyconnell, Tel (049) 26391. Guesthouse owners are experienced in dealing with anglers.

TACKLE SHOPS

Coulston's Tackle Shop, Bawnboy Road, Ballyconnell.
Angler's Rest, Main Street, Ballyconnell.

BAIT

Irish Angling Services, Ardlougher, Ballyconnell,
Tel (049) 26258.

OTHER WATERS IN THIS AREA

See Belturbet, Cavan, Killeshandra, Ballinamore.

SPECIES

Bream, Roach, Hybrids, Perch, Pike, Eels, some Tench, some Rudd.

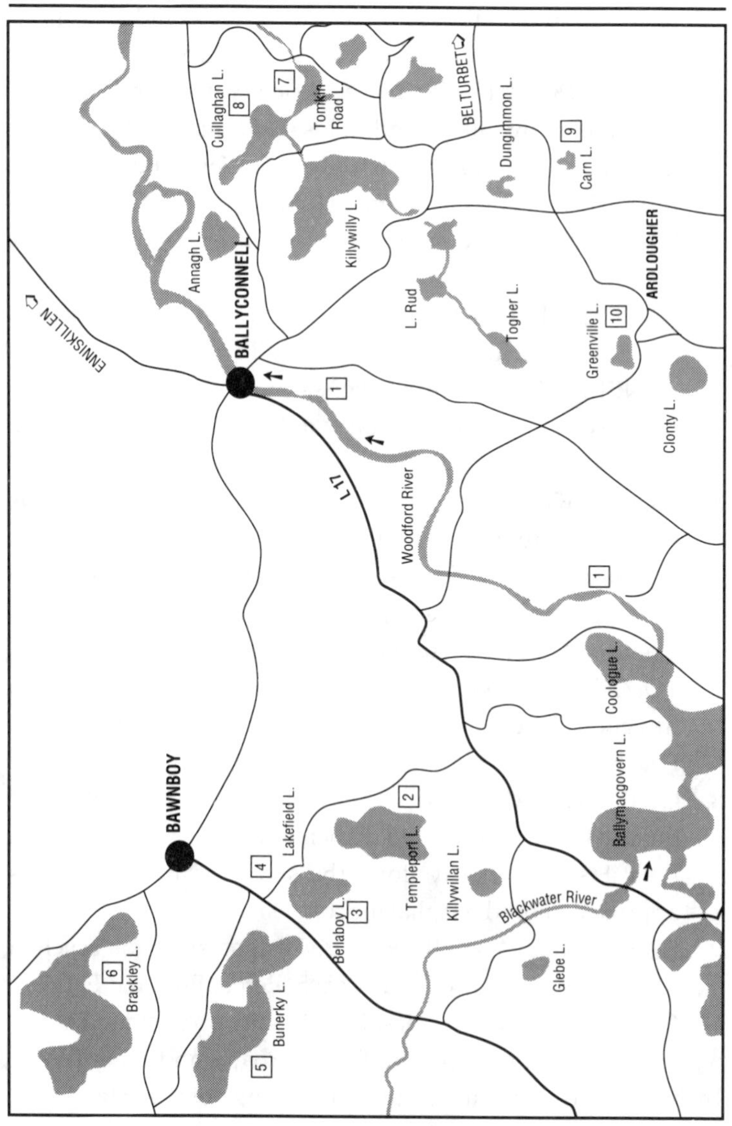

1. WOODFORD RIVER/CANAL: This small canalised river above the town provides good sport for Roach, small Bream, Perch, Pike and some Eels. Access is at many places up to Garadice Lake (see Ballinamore, Co. Leitrim).

Special Note. Major work is in progress on this river, in restoring the canal. Fishing on this water from Ballinamore via Ballyconnell will be affected in many places for some time.

2. TEMPLEPORT LAKE: This is a rich water 3 miles (5 km) from Bawnboy village and holds good quality Bream. This lake also has a stock of Roach, Hybrids, Perch, Pike and Eels.
3. BELLABOY LAKE: One mile (1.5 km) from Bawnboy, this lake provides good sport for Roach, Bream, Hybrids, Pike and Perch.
4. LAKEFIELD LAKE: Near Bawnboy, this is primarily a Roach water with some Bream, Pike, Perch and Eels.
5. BUNERKY LAKE: Near Lakefield, this big open water has good Roach, with some Rudd and quality Hybrids, Perch and Pike.
6. BRACKLEY LAKE: A scenic lake near Bawnboy and beside the Swanlinbar road, this water has a limited stock of Bream which give good sport. It holds some quality Roach and Hybrids, with Perch, Pike and Eels. Access is off the main road to Prospect Point.
7. TOMKIN ROAD LAKE: Access is easy to this water which has good Roach. It also holds some Bream, Hybrids, Rudd, Pike and Eels.
8. CUILLAGHAN LAKE: This water has a good stock of quality Bream, with Rudd, Roach, Hybrids, Pike, Perch and Eels. Fishing is best along the southern bank which is approached off the Aghalane road.
9. CARN LAKE: A small lake, it gives good sport for Tench in May and June. It also holds Roach, Perch, Pike and Eels.
10. GREENVILLE LAKE: Beside Ardlougher, this good water has fishing from stands for Bream, Roach, and some Tench.

In North Co. Cavan, Lough McNean, beside Blacklion, produces good Roach, with some Bream, Pike and Eels.

BELTURBET

Belturbet is situated on the N3 road from Dublin, 8 miles (13 km) north of Cavan town.

It is on the River Erne where the river becomes navigable for cruisers. The town is surrounded by lakes, and the Woodford River enters Lough Erne near here. Bream come on the feed from mid April to October. Roach and Pike fishing is good over most of the year, but the best results come in the colder months. Tench fishing is best in May and June. There is a variety of lakes and rivers in this area.

CLUB

Belturbet Coarse Angling Club.

ANGLING CONTACTS

Guesthouse owners in this area are experienced in dealing with anglers.

TACKLE SHOPS

McMahon's, Bridge Street, Belturbet, Tel (049) 22400.

BAIT

Irish Angling Services, Ardlougher, Ballyconnell, Tel (049) 26258.

McMahon's, Bridge Street, Belturbet, Tel (049) 22400.

Mrs E. Dunne, Hilltop, Kilduff, Belturbet, Tel (049) 22114.

Mrs C. Braiden, Kilduff, Belturbet, Tel (049) 22452.

OTHER WATERS IN THIS AREA

See Ballyconnell, Killeshandra, Cavan.

SPECIES

Bream, Roach, Hybrids, Tench, Perch, Pike, Eels, some Rudd.

COMPETITION

Belturbet Festival. July/August.

BOATS

Sean Fitzpatrick, Putiaghan, Belturbet, Tel (049) 22424.

T. Kennedy, Clooninny, Belturbet, Tel (049) 22355.

D. Carlin, 9 Lee Drive, Belturbet, Tel (049) 22637.

International Fishing Centre, Lough Dooley, Belturbet, Tel (049) 22616.

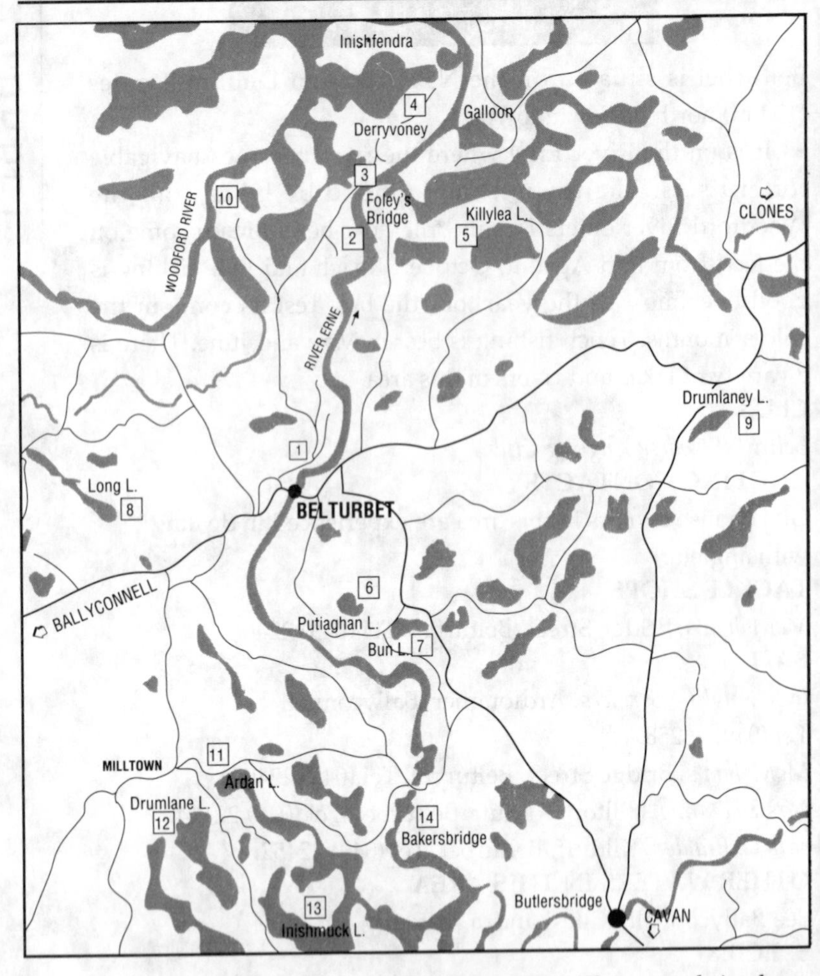

1. RIVER ERNE, CREAMERY STRETCH: This stretch is about 2–5 feet deep and holds Roach, Perch and Bream. Downstream of the jetty and bend, there are Bream as the river widens.
2. RIVER ERNE, CLOONINNY STRETCH: The river here is slow and deep, with good Bream and Roach. This stretch also holds Perch, Pike and Eels. There are some isolated swims up-river towards the town.

3. RIVER ERNE, FOLEY'S BRIDGE: This has a good open bank for Bream and Roach fishing. At the lower end and beside the marker, it is shallow with good Bream at times.
4. LOUGH ERNE, DERRYVONEY: This is a good fishery, with easy access from a car park. There is a good stock of Bream here, fishable from an open bank. This water also holds Roach, Hybrids, Perch, Pike and Eels.
5. KILLYLEA LAKE: Near Castlesaunderson Forest, this lake is a good Bream and Roach fishery. There are also Pike, Perch and Eels here.
6. PUTIAGHAN LAKE: Bream, Roach and Tench abound in this weedy, rich water. The lake is off the Cavan road about 2 miles (3 km) from Belturbet.
7. BUN LAKE: Fishing is from stands on this good lake for Tench, Bream, Perch, Roach and Pike. Access is from the car park beside the Cavan road.
8. LONG LAKE: This water is seldom fished, but the long walk will reward the angler, with good Bream and Roach fishing. This water is off the Ballyconnell road at Killynaher Church.
9. DRUMLANEY LAKE: Beside the Cavan-Clones road, fishing is from stands. The lake holds Bream, Roach, Pike, Perch and Eels.
10. WOODFORD RIVER: A small and slow-moving river with a depth of 6–10 feet, it has Bream and Roach fishing near Teemore Lake. The river is approached to the left off the road leading to Foley's Bridge.

    Special Note: Development work is in progress on this river. Fishing will be affected for some time.
11. ARDAN LAKE: Near Milltown, this lake provides good sport for Bream and Roach, with Pike, Perch, Eels and some Rudd.
12. DRUMLANE LAKE: A rich lake with good-quality Bream and Roach, but it has slow fishing.

13. INISHMUCK LAKE: This water at the causeway produces good catches of Bream and Roach from fairly shallow waters.
14. RIVER ERNE, BAKERSBRIDGE: From just above the bridge to 600 m and downstream, there are pools with some good Bream, Roach, Perch, Hybrids and Eels.

CAVAN

Cavan is situated on the N3 road 70 miles (112 km) north of Dublin. An industrious market town surrounded by low hills, it offers good sports facilities with a golf course, tennis courts and a riding school. Bream and Roach fishing is good from mid April to mid October, with some waters having Roach feeding through most of the cold months. Pike feed all year but are best in the period September to April. Tench fishing is best in May and June. There is a great variety of lakes and rivers in this area.

CLUB

Cavan Tourist Association, Mrs Iris Neill, Lisnamandra, Crossdoney, Cavan, Tel (049) 37196

ANGLING CONTACTS

Hugh Gough, Central Fisheries Board, Cathedral Road, Cavan, Tel (049) 31356.

Guesthouse owners are experienced in dealing with anglers.

TACKLE SHOPS

Fergal Murray, Flying Sportsman, College Street, Cavan.
Sports World, Main Street, Cavan.
Eamon Condon, Sports Shop, Main Street, Cavan.

BAIT

Mrs P. Brady, Blenacup, Cavan, Tel (049) 31513.
Mrs I. Neill, Lisnamandra, Cavan, Tel (049) 37196.
Mrs P. Mundy, Deredis, Cavan, Tel (049) 31427.
Sports World, Main Street, Cavan, Tel (049) 31812.

OTHER WATERS IN THIS AREA

See Belturbet, Killeshandra, Gowna, Arva.

SPECIES

Bream, Roach, Hybrids, Perch, Pike, Eels, Rudd.

CAVAN

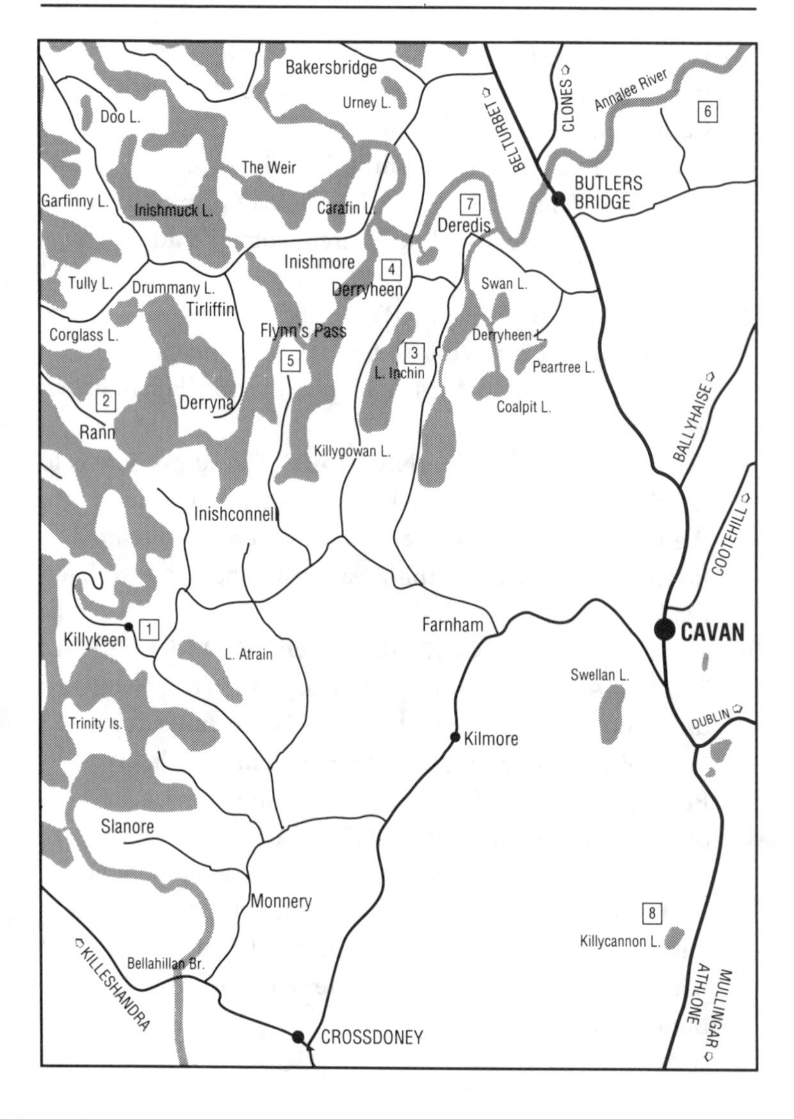

1. LOUGH OUGHTER, KILLYKEEN: A first-class fishing area in Killykeen Forest Park, 5 miles (8 km) west of Cavan. Access and parking are easy, with good clear fishing banks. The match stretch with 60 pegs has good depths at the low numbers and rises to 4 feet (1.2 m) at pegs 50–60. There is a good stock of Bream, Roach, Perch and Pike here.
2. LOUGH OUGHTER, RANN: The best fishing here is opposite the castle where the depth is 16 feet (5 m). Fishing is for good Bream and Roach. This water is approached off the Killeshandra road at Farnham Gates, or near Kilmore Cathedral.
3. LOUGH INCHIN: The fishing here is from two fishing stands into 8 feet (2.4 m). The lake holds Bream, Roach and Tench. There are also Pike, Perch, some Rudd and Eels here.
4. RIVER ANNALEE, DERRYHEEN: Access is over the private land of Mr West. Please ask permission. The deep pool holds Bream to 4 lbs (1.8 kg) with some Perch, Roach and Pike.
5. LOUGH OUGHTER, FLYNN'S PASS: The access here is to the right of the car park and down a steep hill. Fishing is to the right, near the reeds and where there are Bream and Roach. The approach to this area is from the Cavan to Rann road.
6. RIVER ANNALEE, CURRAGHANOE AND KNOCKFAD, BALLYHAISE: This is a 50 peg match stretch which has a deep pool (35 feet/10 m) at the top. The average depth is 6 feet (1.8 m) with a moderate flow. Bream, Roach, Hybrids, Perch, Pike and Eels are found here. This area is approached from the Cavan-Ballyhaise road.
7. RIVER ANNALEE, DEREDIS: This has a deep pool below the fast water which holds some Trout. The pool has eddies with submerged hazards. It holds good Roach with some Bream. This stretch is to the west of the Cavan-Butlersbridge road.

8. KILLYCANNON LAKE: This is a small water beside the Cavan-Ballinagh road 3 miles (4.8 km) from Cavan. There is parking along a busy road. Fishing is from a stand and from the area beside the rock. This area has some Tench to 4 lbs (1.8 kg) and the water also holds some Roach, Rudd, small Bream, Pike and Eels.
9. LAVEY LAKE: Alongside the Dublin road, this lake with easy access has a good stock of Roach, with Pike and Eels. Seven miles from Cavan, this lake is not shown on the map.

COOTEHILL

Cootehill is situated on the Cavan-Carrickmacross road near the Co. Monaghan border about 16 miles (25 km) north-east of Cavan. It is a busy market town on the rivers Annalee and Dromore. Bream fishing is good from mid April to October. Roach and Pike are good throughout the year, but the best results come in the colder months. Tench fishing is best in May and June. The fishing here is in lakes and rivers.

CLUB

Cootehill Tourist Development Association.
Mrs Vera Greenan, The Beeches, Station Road, Cootehill,
Tel (049) 52307

ANGLING CONTACTS

Guesthouse owners are experienced in dealing with anglers.

TACKLE SHOPS

Liam Hayes, General Shop, Main Street, Cootehill.

BAIT

C.J. Fay, Cabragh House, Cootehill, Tel (049) 52153.
Mrs Eileen Smith, Hillview House, Corick, Cootehill,
Tel (049) 53039.

OTHER WATERS IN THIS AREA
See Cavan, Ballybay, Cootehill, Belturbet, Clones, Carrickmacross.

SPECIES
Bream, Roach, Hybrids, some Rudd, Tench, Perch, Pike, Eels.

COMPETITIONS
Cootehill Angling Festival, September

BOATS
C.J. Fay, Cabragh House, Cootehill, Tel (049) 52153.
Mrs U. Smith, Riverside, Cootehill, Tel (049) 52150.

COOTEHILL

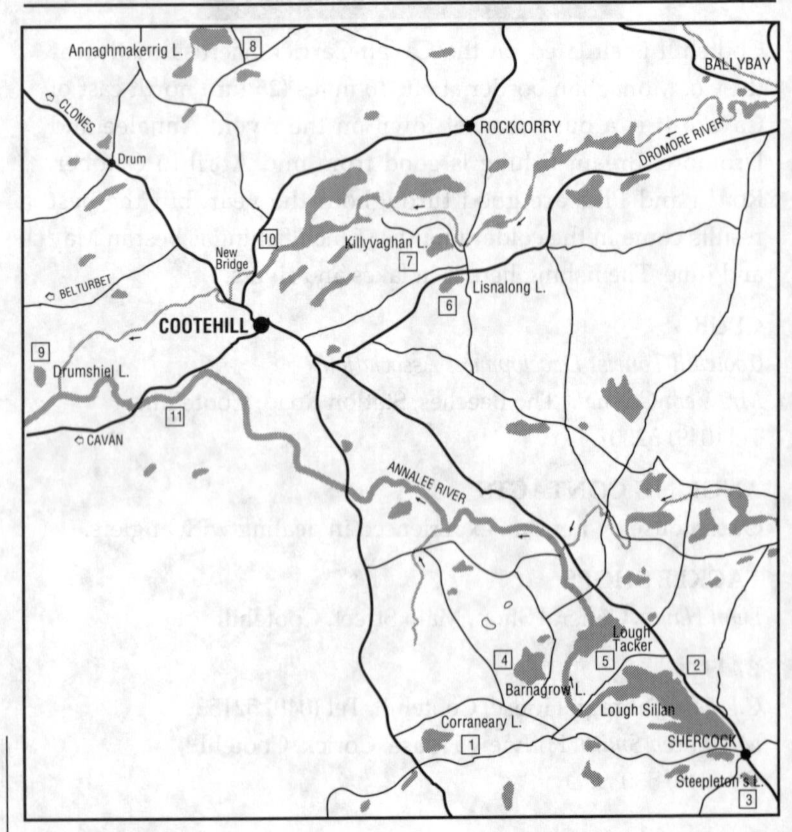

1. CORRANEARY LAKE (CHURCH LAKE): This is a good water with Bream to 5 lbs (2.2 kg). It also has Roach, Perch and Pike. About 3 miles (5 km) from Shercock, this lake has access opposite the church.
2. LOUGH SILLAN, SHERCOCK: This big lake beside Shercock holds good-quality Roach. It also has some Bream, with Perch, Pike and Eels. Fishing is beside the village and also at Annaghfarney, near the car park.
3. STEEPLETON'S LAKE: In Shercock, this muddy-bottomed lake produces Tench in May and June.
4. BARNAGROW LAKE: Under steep hills, this lake with its many bays holds a good stock of Bream which are localised. It also has Roach, Hybrids, Perch, Pike, and Eels.
5. LOUGH TACKER: This is a fair fishery for Bream, with an abundance of Perch. It also holds Roach and small Pike.
6. LISNALONG LAKE: Parking is beside the Ballybay-Cootehill road. This lake, with reeds and soft margins, has some good swims for Bream to 4 lbs (1.8 kg), Roach, Perch, Pike and also good Tench to 5 lbs (2.2 kg).
7. KILLYVAGHAN LAKE: A big lake, off the Ballybay road, with the best fishing under the hill. Fishing for Bream here can be very localised. It also holds Roach, Perch, Pike and Eels.
8. ANNAGHMAKERRIG LAKE: A big lake, off the Cootehill-Newbliss road, which caters for 60 anglers in match conditions. A good fishery, it has easy access and is suitable for disabled anglers. Fishing is from good banks for Roach, Roach-Bream Hybrids, some Bream, quality Perch, Pike and Eels.
9. DRUMSHIEL LAKE: A small lake under a hill, it gives good sport for Bream, Roach, Hybrids, Pike and Eels. Access is off the Cootehill-Belturbet road.
10. DROMORE RIVER: A shallow water, which is weedy in summer. Roach fishing is best in the winter. Above Ballynascarvagh Bridge, there is a deep pool with Bream.

11. ANNALEE RIVER: Beside the Cavan road, the river here at Corick has some swims which hold Roach, small Bream, Perch and Pike.

GOWNA

Gowna is situated near the Longford border just south of Arva. The Lough Gowna complex is at the top of the River Erne system. Bream fishing is excellent and stretches from mid April to October. Roach, Perch and Pike provide good sport throughout the year, but the colder months produce the best fish. Tench fishing is from May to July. The waters here also hold Trout and the Upper Erne AC requests anglers to return all fish alive. There is a variety of lakes and a river to fish here.

CLUB

Lough Gowna Anglers Club, John F. Smyth, Glenbrook, Gowna, Tel (043) 83183.

ANGLING CONTACTS

Alan Sloane, Post Office, Gowna, Tel (043) 83101.
Guesthouse owners are experienced in dealing with anglers.

TACKLE SHOPS

Sloane's, Post Office, Gowna, Tel (043) 83101.

BAIT

Mrs F. Kinkade, Lakeside, Gowna, Tel (043) 83242.

OTHER WATERS IN THIS AREA

See Arva, Carrigallen, Killeshandra, Cavan.

SPECIES

Bream, Roach, Hybrids, Perch, Tench, Pike, Eels.

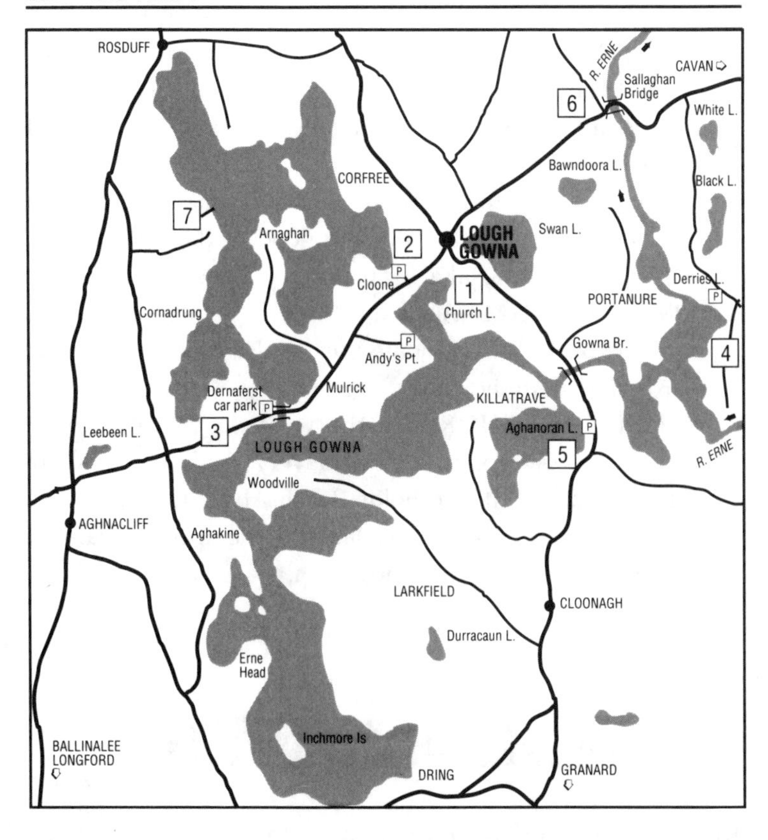

1. CHURCH LAKE: A good stretch with easy access and parking just at the village. Fishing into deep water for Roach and Hybrids, with some Bream and Perch.
2. CLOONE LAKE: Fishing is to the left up from the island, about half a mile from the village. It holds good Bream to 5 lbs (2.2 kg) but shoals are few. The area is good for Roach, Perch, Pike and Eels.
3. DERNAFERST, LOUGH GOWNA: There is an amenity area here with good parking. Fishing is best in the lake facing west, with Bream and Roach along the stretch for 330 yards (300 m). Just one and a half miles from the village, this lake is beside the Longford road.

4. DERRIES LAKE: This is a good water in the early and late seasons. To the left, from the bay at the first car park, there is first-class fishing for Bream in May/June. Near the big rock at the point, there is also good Bream fishing. This lake is approached off the Cavan road at two and a half miles from Gowna.
5. AGHANORAN LAKE: Access is from the lakeside car park on the Granard road. Fishing is good to the right, where the river leaves the lake, for Bream and Roach.
6. RIVER ERNE, SALLAGHAN BRIDGE: Some good swims upriver for Roach and some Bream, also downriver at 220 yards (200 m) in the pool.
7. STRETTON'S SHORE: In the western part of Lough Gowna, this is a good stretch with very good Bream fishing into deep water. It also holds Roach, Hybrids, Perch, Pike and Eels. Fishing is also available on the opposite bank at Rosduff, for good Bream and Roach.

KILLESHANDRA

Killeshandra is situated on the Cavan to Carrick-on-Shannon road, 11 miles (17 km) from Cavan town. This is a small industrious town surrounded by the waters of the River Erne. Bream and Roach fishing is good from mid April to October, and Pike fishing is good throughout the year, although it is more productive in the colder months. Fishing is in lakes and rivers here.

CLUB

Killeshandra Holidays, Mrs Kathleen Bothwell, Killeshandra, Tel (049) 34149.

Killeshandra Anglers Club, Sean McMahon, Main Street, Tel (049) 34438.

ANGLING CONTACTS

Guesthouse owners are experienced in dealing with anglers.

TACKLE SHOPS

McMahon's, Hunting and Fishing Shop, Main Street, Killeshandra, Tel (049) 34438.

BAIT

McMahon's, Main Street, Killeshandra, Tel (049) 34438.

OTHER WATERS IN THIS AREA

See Cavan, Carrigallen, Belturbet, Gowna, Arva.

SPECIES

Bream, Roach, Hybrids, Perch, Pike, Eels.

BOATS

Mrs T. Farrelly, Snakiel, Killeshandra, Tel (049) 34197.

1. TOWN LAKE: Access is from the car park at the waterside. Bream and Roach are common here, close to the town along the Belturbet road.
2. CASTLE RIVER-NEW BRIDGE RIVER: A small river with an abundance of small Roach which provide good sport in the colder months of the year. Fishing is along the Belturbet road at New Bridge and the river is also accessible to the right off the Killykeen Forest road.
3. TULLYGUIDE LAKE: On the road to Lough Oughter, this lake on the right, 2 miles (3 km) from the town, has easy parking and access. A good fishery for Bream, Roach, Perch, Pike and Eels. Access is good for disabled anglers.
4. LOUGH OUGHTER-GORTANOUL: Approached off the Belturbet road, this fishery is in the Killykeen Forest Park. The area at the Sandy Point is good for Bream to 4 lbs (1.8 kg). Parking is at the waterside.
5. LOUGH OUGHTER-KILLYKEEN: The best fishing here is along the well-marked match stretch. Fishing is good at the first pegs, also in the middle and towards the top end. Fishing here is for good Bream, with some Roach, Hybrids, Perch and Pike.

KILLESHANDRA

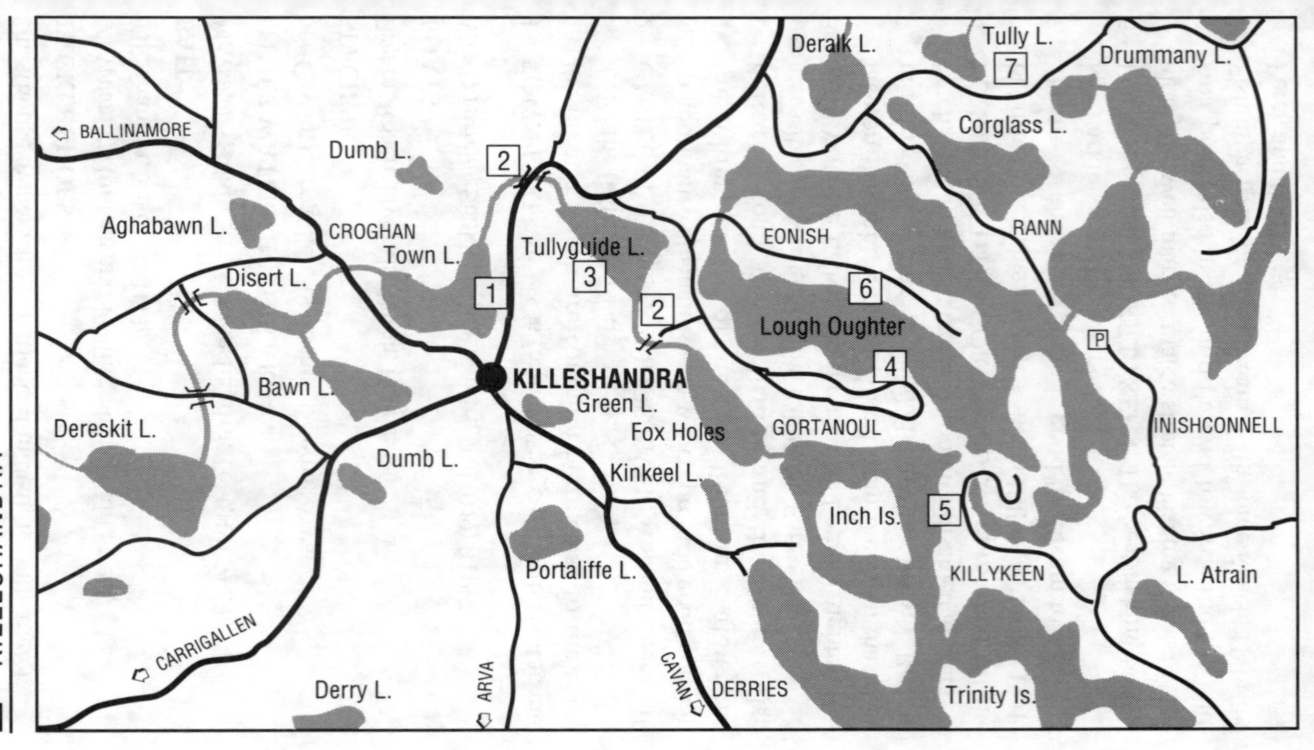

6. LOUGH OUGHTER-EONISH: This stretch fishes 60 anglers in a match. It has a good stock of Roach, Hybrids, Bream and small Perch, with Pike. The approach is to the left off the Killykeen Forest park road.
7. TULLY LAKE: Fishing here is from stands. Heavy baiting is essential on this slow-fishing water for Bream to 6 lbs (2.7 kg). The lake is off the Butlersbridge road at 3.5 miles (5.6 km) and to the left.

   Note: For other waters near Killeshandra, see Cavan and Belturbet.

KINGSCOURT

Kingscourt is situated in east Co. Cavan on the Bailieborough-Carrickmacross road, near counties Meath and Monaghan. It is a busy town 50 miles (80 km) from Dublin. Bream fishing comes on in mid April and continues to October. Roach, Perch and Pike fishing is good during the summer, but it is during the colder months that the Roach and Pike are at their best. Tench fishing is good in the summer, with May/June being the best period. In this area, fishing is in lakes.

CLUB

Kingscourt Angling and Tourism Association.
Mrs Maureen Campbell, Corlea, Kingscourt, Tel (042) 67316.

ANGLING CONTACTS

Guesthouse owners are experienced in dealing with anglers.

TACKLE SHOPS

W.A. Sheckleton, General Shop, Main Street, Kingscourt.
Gerald Mackin, Church Street, Kingscourt.
Jimmy McMahon, Carrick Sports, Carrickmacross,
Tel (042) 61714.

BAIT

Jimmy McMahon, Carrick Sports, Carrickmacross, Tel (042) 61714.

OTHER WATERS IN THIS AREA

See Carrickmacross, Drumconrath, Bailieborough, Shercock.

SPECIES

Roach, Bream, Hybrids, Perch, Rudd, Pike, Tench, Eels.

KINGSCOURT

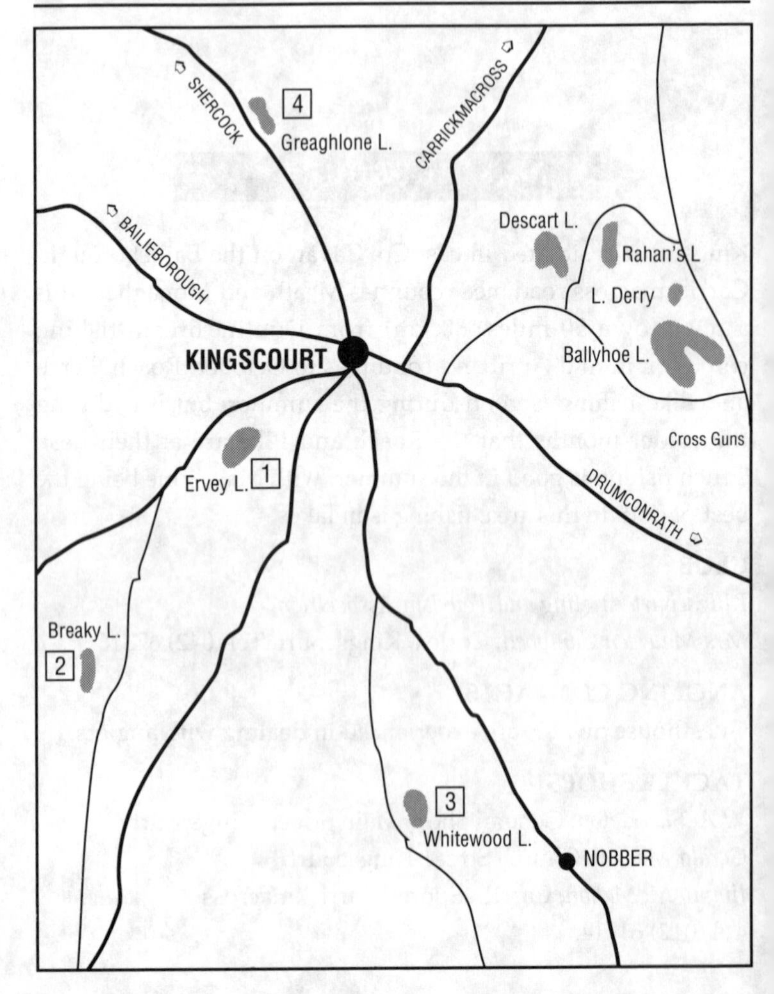

1. ERVEY LAKE: This 44 acre lake is a short distance from Kingscourt and has good parking facilities. The water holds good quality Roach, Bream, Roach/Bream Hybrids, Perch, Pike and Eels.
2. BREAKY LAKE: This water of 27 acres has Perch and Pike, some Bream and Rudd. Good access and parking are available at the southern shore.
3. WHITEWOOD LAKE: A 77 acre lake near Kilmainham Wood, it has waterside parking. The margins are shallow and weedy, but good results for Roach and Bream can come from the area to the left of the car park.
4. GREAGHLONE LAKE: Beside the Shercock road, this lake holds good Roach, with Perch, Pike and Eels. Beside this water is Cornalara Lake, which is reeded and holds good Roach.

Note: For Descart L., Ballyhoe L. etc., see Carrickmacross.

VIRGINIA

Virginia is situated on the Dublin-Cavan road (N3) about 16 miles (25 km) south-east of Cavan. Virginia is a tidy town, located on the banks of Lough Ramor. Bream fishing is good from April to late October. Roach and Pike are good most times, but it is during the winter that the Roach and Pike are best. In this area, fishing is in lakes and a river.

CLUB

Virginia Development Association.

ANGLING CONTACTS

Ray Arnold, Main Street, Virginia, Tel (049) 47060.
Guesthouse owners are experienced in dealing with anglers.

TACKLE SHOPS

Arnold's Shop, Main Street, Virginia.

BAIT

Arnold's Shop, Main Street, Virginia, Tel (049) 47060.

OTHER WATERS IN THIS AREA

See Bailieborough, Cavan, Gowna.

SPECIES

Roach, Bream, Hybrids, Perch, Pike, Eels, Rudd.

VIRGINIA

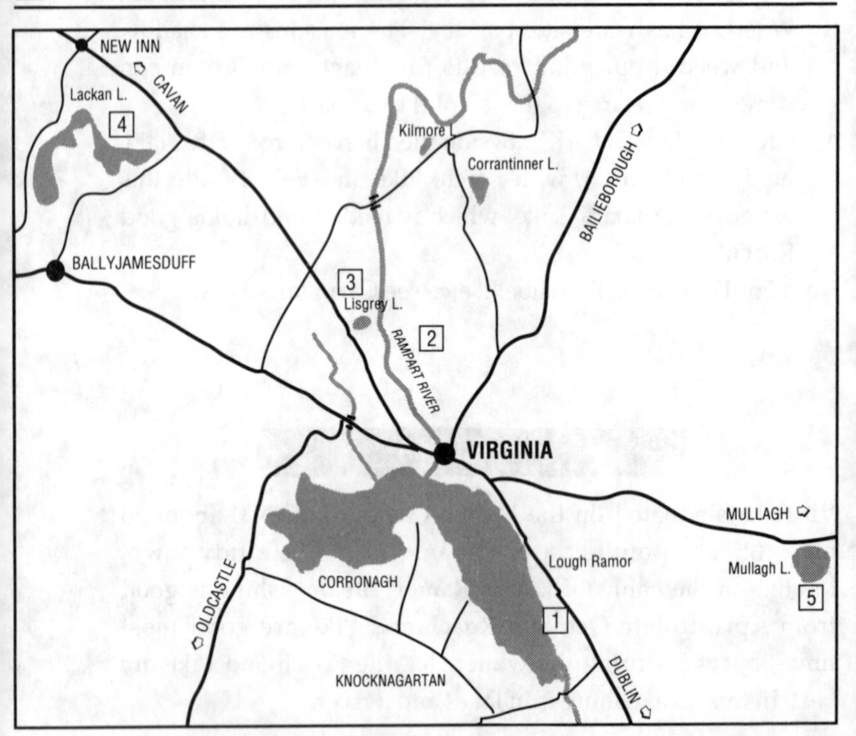

1. LOUGH RAMOR: This is a big lake of over 1500 acres along the N3 road. Near the town, there are facilities for parking and for boat access. The margins are often shallow and rocky. In May and June, Bream can be caught along the rocky shoreline from the town's golf course, south to the milk factory. When water conditions are right, there is good fishing at the caravan park and below the lake outflow at Blackwater Bridge.

Along the south-western shore at Knocknagartan, there is great Bream and Roach fishing. Access is over private property and permission should always be sought. At Knocknagartan, the fishing facilities are perfect for disabled anglers. Camping is not allowed here and anglers are asked to remove all litter.

On the western side at Corronagh Forest, there are also a few swims for Bream and Roach. This lake also holds some Brown Trout.

2. RAMPART RIVER: There is a short, quiet stretch of this river, with access from the ball alley, which has some Bream, Roach and Perch. This lake also holds some Brown Trout.
3. LISGREY LAKE: Beside the Cavan road, fishing is from stands for some Bream, Roach and Pike.
4. NADREEGEEL (LACKAN) LAKES: Situated about 2 miles (3.2 km) from Ballyjamesduff, these lakes are connected by a narrow and heavily-weeded channel. The upper (western) lake is approached from the Virginia-Cavan road. Parking is limited along this narrow road and there are some swims which can be fished. The lake holds good stocks of Roach, Rudd, Hybrids, Pike, Perch and Eels. Nadreegeel is locally called Lackan Lake.

   The lower lake has limited fishing space and is approached off the Virginia-Cavan road near the Billises. There are Bream, Roach, Pike, Perch and Eels here.
5. MULLAGH LAKE: Near Mullagh village, this lake is beside the Virginia road. There is parking near the water and fishing is into about 8 feet (2.4 m). Fishing is for Roach, Perch and Pike.

County Clare

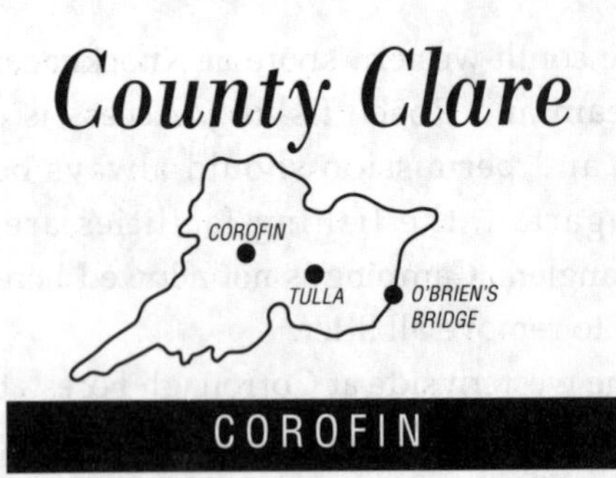

COROFIN

Corofin is located about 9 miles (14 km) north-west of Ennis. This is a small village on the River Fergus, with Trout and coarse fishing waters nearby. There is limited Bream fishing here which provides sport during the summer months. Rudd to specimen size feed freely during the summer. Tench fishing is good from mid May to September. Perch and Pike are also present, with winter Pike fishing producing the best fish. Fishing in this area is in lakes.

CLUB

There is no local angling club in Corofin.

ANGLING CONTACTS

Michael Cleary, Shannon Regional Fisheries Board, Corofin, Tel (065) 27657.

For information west of this area, contact Mrs D. Griffey, Lahardan House, Crusheen, Tel (065) 27128.

Guesthouse owners are experienced in dealing with anglers.

TACKLE SHOPS

Burke's Shop, Main Street.

BAIT

Joe Maloney, Riverside House, O'Brien's Bridge, Tel (061) 377303.

OTHER WATERS IN THIS AREA

See Tulla.

SPECIES

Rudd, Tench, Perch, Pike, Bream, Eels.

BOATS

Shannon Fisheries Board: Michael Cleary, Ennis Road, Tel (065) 27657.

Burke's Shop, Main Street.

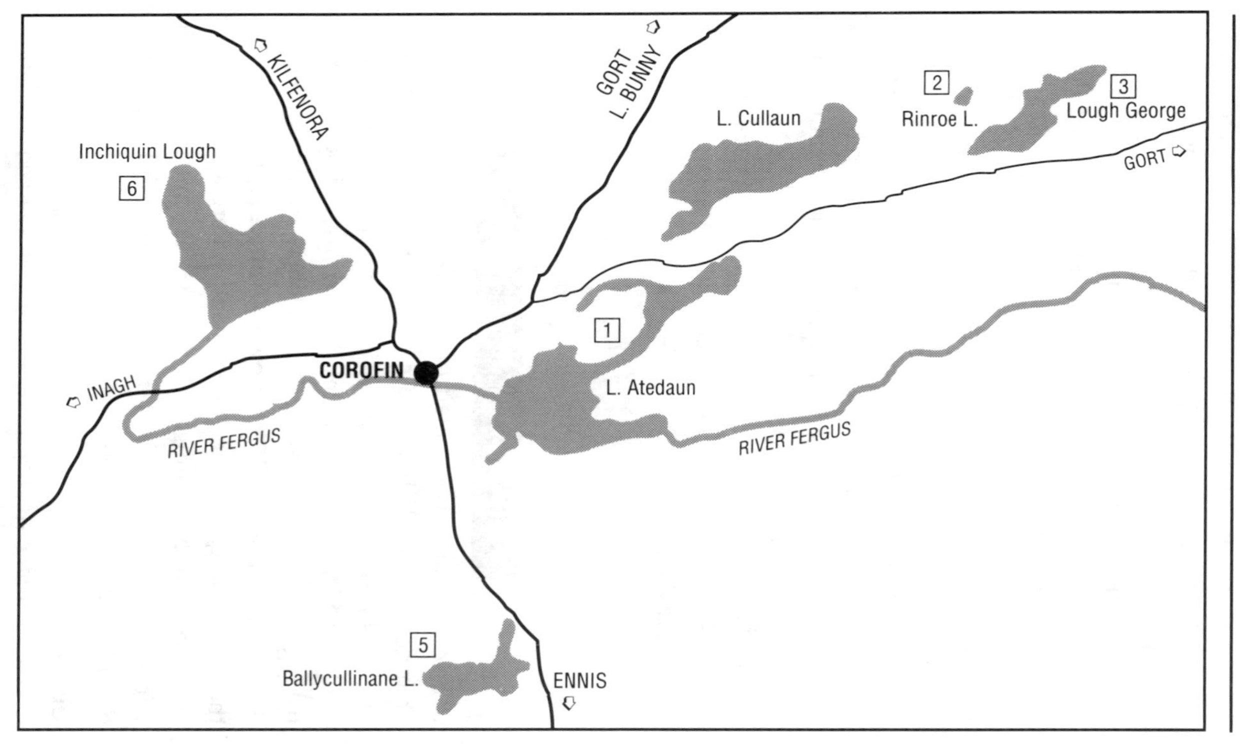

KILFENORA
GORT L. BUNNY
L. Cullaun
2 Rinroe L.
3 Lough George
GORT
Inchiquin Lough 6
1
COROFIN
L. Atedaun
INAGH
RIVER FERGUS
RIVER FERGUS
5 Ballycullinane L.
ENNIS

1. ATEDAUN LAKE: This is a big exposed lake and in summer, a very weedy water. It holds good stocks of specimen Rudd, Tench, Pike, Perch and Eels. This lake is best fished from a boat.
2. RINROE LAKE: North of Corofin, this is a small lake which holds specimen Tench, with some Rudd and Perch.
3. LOUGH GEORGE: A big water, there are some Rudd, Perch and Pike here.
4. LOUGH BUNNY: An open lake, it holds Pike, Perch and Rudd.
5. BALLYCULLINANE LAKE: Near Corofin, this lake is best fished from a boat. It holds Bream, Rudd, Perch, Pike and Eels. There is a good stock of quality Rudd/Bream Hybrids with some big Bream in this lake.
6. INCHIQUIN LOUGH: A big and interesting water which holds a good stock of Perch and Rudd. Also produces good Pike fishing.

O'BRIEN'S BRIDGE

O'Brien's Bridge is situated on the west bank of the River Shannon on the Killaloe-Limerick road (R463). O'Brien's Bridge is a small village downriver from the Parteen Dam on the River Shannon and 9 miles (14 km) from Limerick. Bream fishing is good from mid April to October. Rudd feed freely in the summer months. Roach, now present, feed all year, while the best fishing is in the colder months. Perch and Pike give good sport in the summer and the best Pike are caught in the winter. Tench fishing is best in May and June. Fishing is in the River Shannon and lakes.

CLUB

O'Brien's Bridge Angling Club, Joe Maloney, Riverside House, Tel (061) 377303.

O'BRIEN'S BRIDGE

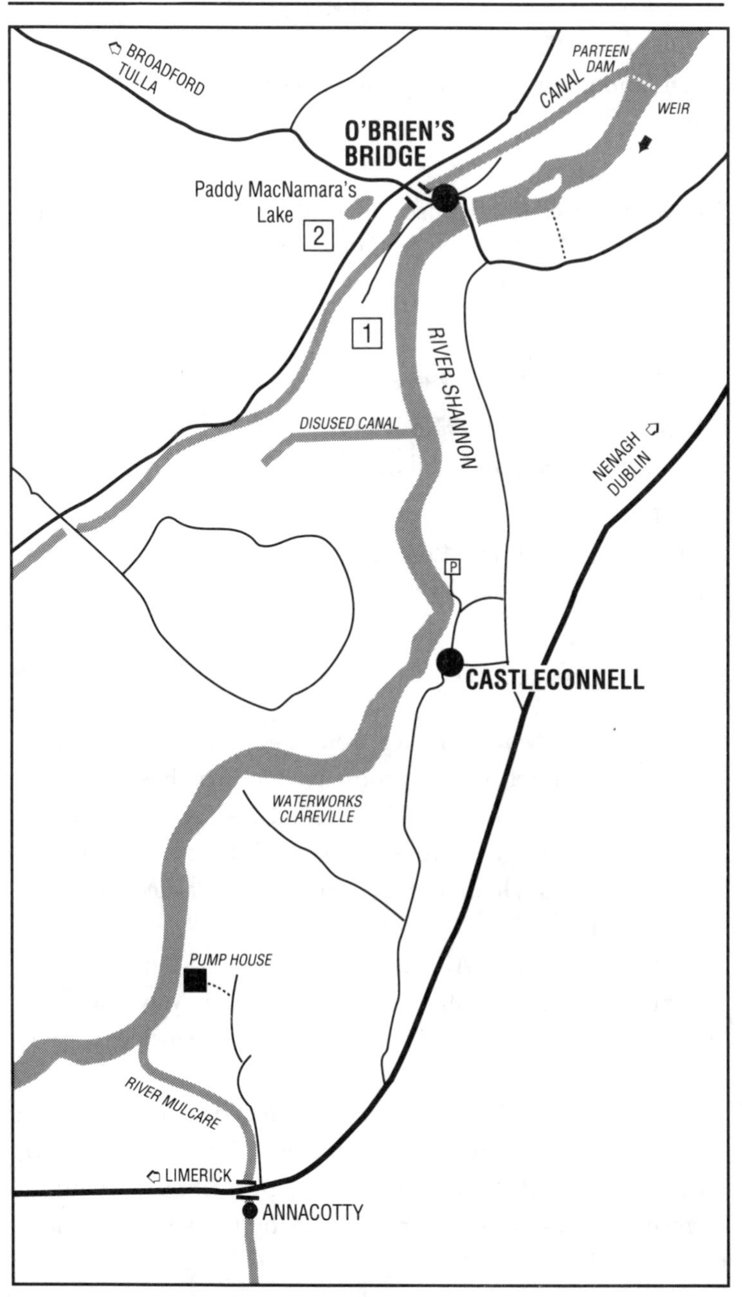

ANGLING CONTACTS

Joe Maloney, Riverside House, O'Brien's Bridge, Tel (061) 377303.

Hotels and guesthouse owners are experienced in dealing with anglers.

TACKLE SHOPS

Joe Maloney, Riverside House, O'Brien's Bridge, Tel (061) 377303.
Jim Robinson, Tackle Shop, Thomond Shopping Centre, Limerick, (061) 44900.

BAIT

Joe Maloney, Riverside House, O'Brien's Bridge.

OTHER WATERS IN THIS AREA

See Portumna/Killaloe, Tulla, Limerick.

SPECIES

Bream, Rudd, Hybrids, Roach, Perch, Pike, Eels, Tench, some Carp.

BOATS

Joe Maloney, Riverside House, O'Brien's Bridge.

1. RIVER SHANNON: Down from the Parteen Dam, there is a match stretch which produces good catches of Bream, Perch, Rudd, Roach and Eels. Good Pike are also present. Below the bridge, there is also good fishing for Bream and other species. The river then continues to Castleconnell (see Limerick).
2. PADDY MacNAMARA'S LAKE: Beside the Limerick road, this lake holds small Rudd and Perch. In May and June, there is Tench fishing. There is also a small stock of Carp in this water.

Special Note: The River Shannon is a mixed fishery, holding Salmon and Trout with coarse fish. The ESB controls this river, which has private stretches, and anglers should acquaint themselves with those waters. Permission to fish is obtainable from the ESB.

TULLA

Tulla is situated about 10 miles (16 km) east of Ennis on the R462 road. This is a small town in the heart of the East Clare Lakes. There are many good quality coarse fishing waters within easy distance of the town. Bream fishing is good from mid April to October. Rudd are at their best in the summer months. Tench feed freely in May and June and again in September. Pike fishing is good all year and the colder months produce the bigger fish. There are some Roach in this area now. Fishing is in lakes here.

CLUB

Tulla & District AC, Brian Culloo, Tulla, Tel (065) 25110.

ANGLING CONTACTS

Brian Culloo, Tulla, Tel (065) 25110.

Guesthouse owners are experienced in dealing with anglers.

TACKLE SHOPS

Joe Maloney, Riverside House, O'Brien's Bridge,
Tel (061) 377303

Jim Robinson, Tackle Shop, Thomond Shopping Centre,
Limerick, Tel (061) 44900

BAIT

Joe Maloney, Riverside House, O'Brien's Bridge.

WATERS FISHED

Lakes.

OTHER WATERS IN THIS AREA

See O'Brien's Bridge, Limerick.

SPECIES

Bream, Rudd, Roach, Hybrids, Tench, Perch, Pike, Eels.

BOATS

Niall O'Donnell, Lake View House, Broadford, Tel (061) 73125.

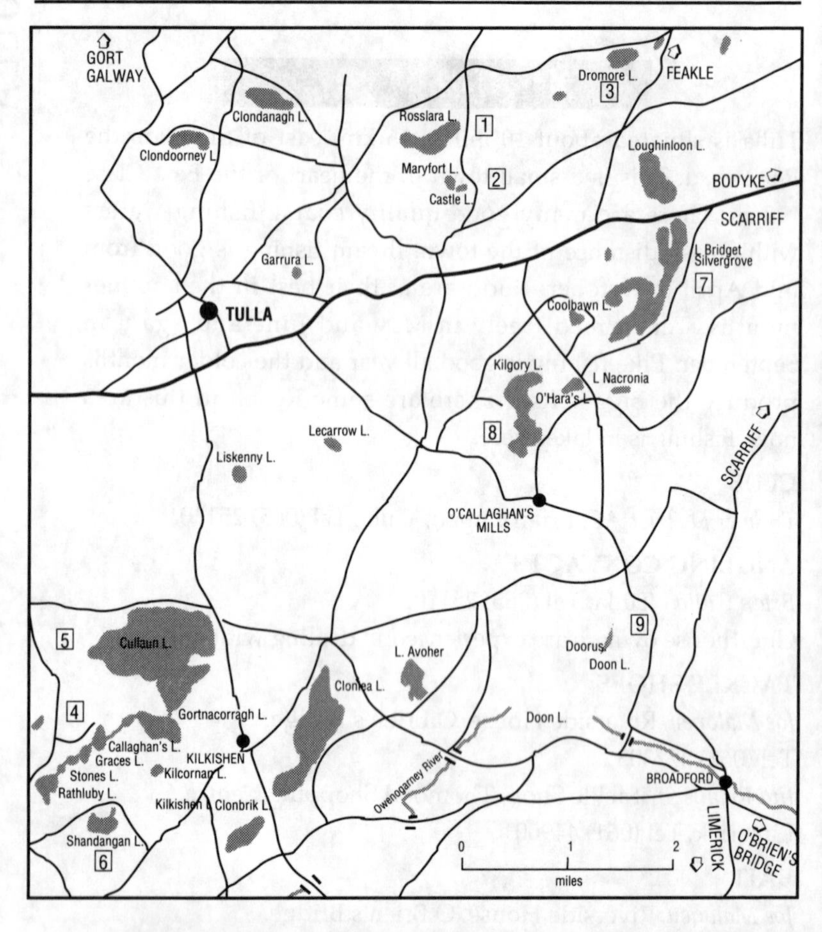

1. ROSSLARA LAKE: This reeded lake, 4 miles (6 km) from Tulla, has a big stock of Rudd, with Bream, Rudd/Bream Hybrids, Perch, Pike and Eels. There are also good Tench to 6 lbs (2.7 kg) in the weedy corners of this lake.
2. MARYFORT AND CASTLE LAKES: These are small lakes which have good fishing for Rudd and Perch, with some Bream and Hybrids. Castle Lake has some Tench to 4 lbs (1.8 kg). The lakes are approached off the Tulla-Bodyke road at 3 miles (5 km) from Tulla.

3. DROMORE LAKE: There is easy access to this water beside the Tulla-Feakle road. It is heavily reeded and is best fished from a boat. It has a good stock of Bream to 4 lbs (1.8 kg) with Rudd, Perch, Pike and Eels.
4. CULLAUN CHAIN: These are four lakes near the Tulla-Kilkishen road which are rich with quality Bream, Rudd and Tench. Stones, Graces and Rathluby lakes fish well, especially for big Tench in May and June. Stones Lake is noted for its quality Tench, with some Bream to specimen size.
5. CULLAUN LAKE: This is a lake of 400 acres close to Quin. It is mainly a good Pike water, but it also contains Bream, Rudd, Hybrids, Perch and Eels.
6. SHANDANGAN LAKE: This is a good water for Rudd, with some Bream. It has a shallow pond nearby which holds good Tench to 5 lbs (2.2 kg).
7. SILVERGROVE/BRIDGET LAKE: Fishing is good on this rich water at several places. Access is easy with good car parking. The lake has a fine stock of Bream to 5 lbs (2.2 kg), Tench to 6 lbs (2.7 kg), Rudd, Perch, Pike and Eels. This excellent water is beside the Tulla/Scarriff road.
8. KILGORY LAKE: This is a reeded lake of 60 acres with a rich stock of Rudd, Bream, Rudd/Bream Hybrids, Perch, Pike and Eels. The lake is approached off the Bodyke road at 4 miles (6 km).
9. DOON LAKE: This water, 1 mile (1.6 km) from Broadford, is in two sections and has an abundance of small Bream, Roach, Rudd, Hybrids, Perch and Pike. Access along the O'Donnell Shore and Creamery Shore is easy, while access to the Doorus Shore is down a steep hill. There is a small stock of Dace in this lake.

County Cork

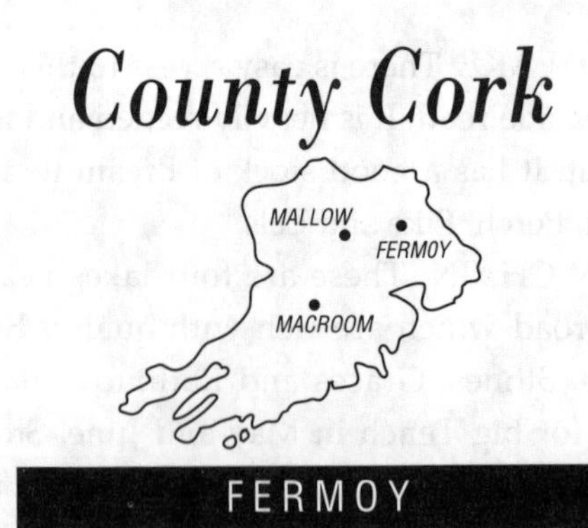

FERMOY

Fermoy straddles the River Blackwater in north-east Co. Cork and is on the Portlaoise-Cork road (N8). It is a busy town in the scenic Blackwater Valley. This is a good angling river. Roach and Dace are at their best in the colder months of the year, though they will also feed during the summer when they provide good sport. Coarse fishing in this area is in the River Blackwater only.

CLUB

Fermoy Coarse Angling Club, Ms Theresa Lawlor, Corrin View Estate, Fermoy, Tel (025) 32074

ANGLING CONTACT

Jack O'Sullivan, 4 Patrick Street, Fermoy, Tel (025) 31110.
Hotel and guesthouse owners are experienced in dealing with anglers.

TACKLE SHOPS

Jack O'Sullivan, 4 Patrick Street.
Brian Twomey, Sports Shop, McCurtain Street, Fermoy.

BAIT

Jack O'Sullivan, 4 Patrick Street.

SPECIES

Roach, Dace, Perch, and some Pike.

RIVER BLACKWATER: Above the town (Barnane), the river is deep and holds adequate stocks of good-quality Roach and Dace. There is access here for disabled anglers.

The fast, shallow water downstream of the bridge fishes well for Roach and Dace from April to June. Opposite the hospital, there is deep water holding large stocks of slightly smaller fish. Further downriver in the Championship Stretch, large Perch are sometimes caught in addition to Roach and Dace.

All these waters are accessible and banks are well kept.

FERMOY

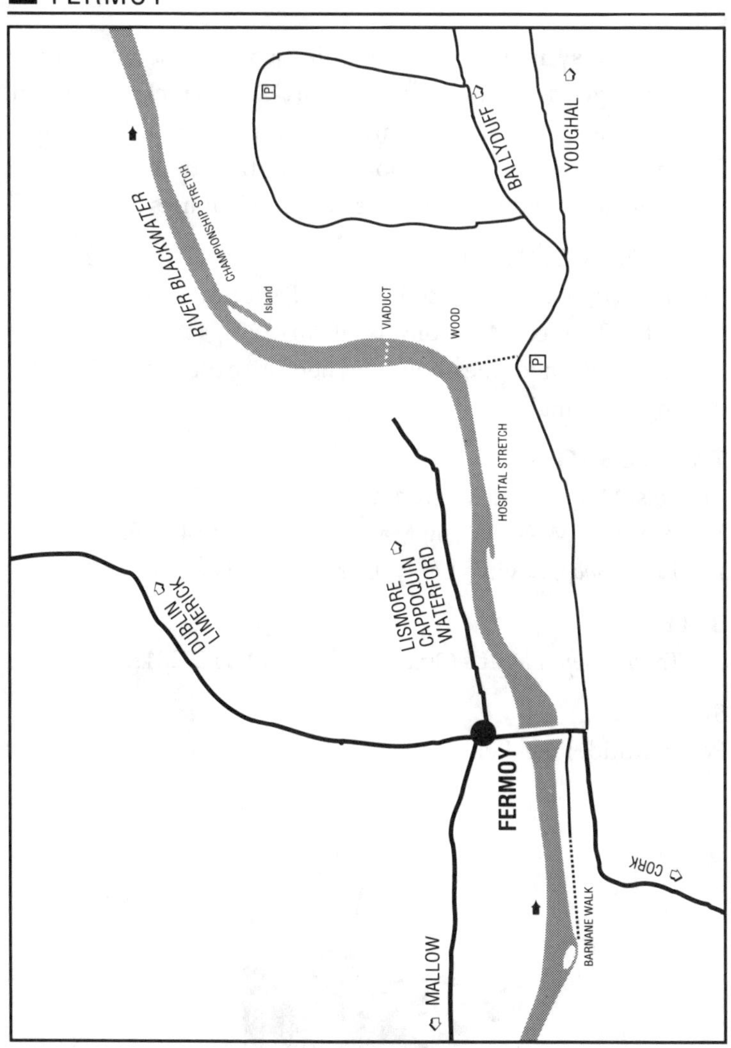

MACROOM

Macroom, in the west of the county, close to the River Lee and lakes, is on the Cork-Killarney road (N22) 24 miles from Cork City.

It is a busy market town, beside two big reservoirs. Pike fishing is good throughout the year. Good stocks of Bream have appeared in the Inniscarra Reservoir. Rudd, Perch and Tench also provide good sport during the summer. Fishing here is in lakes and the River Lee and its tributaries.

ANGLING CONTACTS

Noel Hackett, South Western Regional Fisheries Board,
1 Nevilles Terrace, Macroom, Tel (026) 41221, 41892.
The local hotel and guesthouse owners are experienced in dealing with anglers.

TACKLE SHOPS

Golden's, Main Street, Macroom, Tel (026) 41753.
Tom Sweeney, Masseytown, Macroom, Tel (026) 41566.
The Tackle Shop, Lavitt's Quay, Cork, Tel (021) 272842.

BAIT

The Tackle Shop, Lavitt's Quay, Cork, Tel (021) 272842.

SPECIES

Perch, Rudd, Pike, Eels, some Tench and Bream.

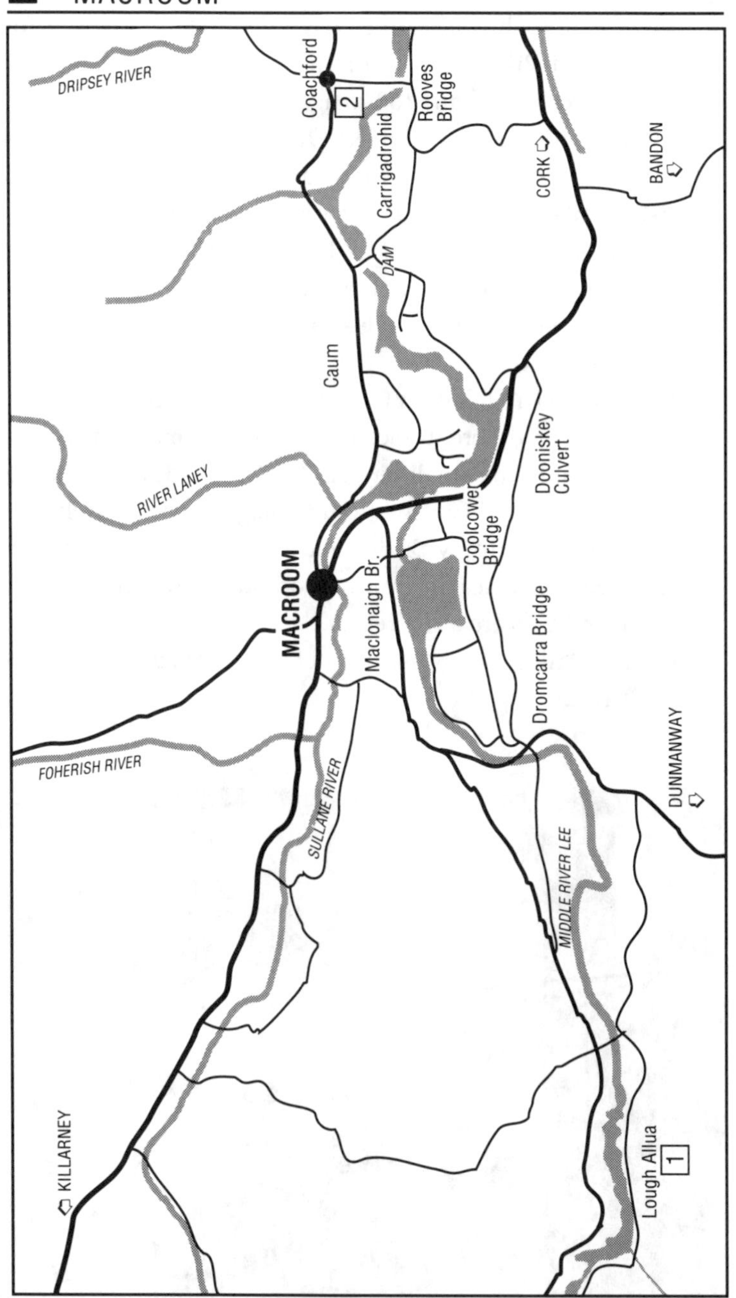
DRIPSEY RIVER
Coachford
2
Rooves Bridge
Carrigadrohid
DAM
CORK
BANDON
Caum
RIVER LANEY
Dooniskey Culvert
Coolcower Bridge
MACROOM
Maclonaigh Br.
Dromcarra Bridge
DUNMANWAY
FOHERISH RIVER
SULLANE RIVER
MIDDLE RIVER LEE
KILLARNEY
Lough Allua
1

1. LOUGH ALLUA: 10 miles (16 km) south-west of Macroom, the scenic Inchigeela Lakes have good shore angling for Perch and Pike. The River Lee flows on from here by Drumcarra Bridge and to Carrigadrohid reservoir.
2. CARRIGADROHID RESERVOIR: Beside Macroom, this water holds good Pike, Rudd and Perch. Recommended fishing sites include Coolcower Bridge, Maclonaigh Bridge, Dooniskey, Caum and the lower reaches of the River Sullane. Rudd and Tench are available in McCulls and Buckley's Ponds, three miles east of Macroom and off the Carrigadrohid Road.
3. INNISCARRA RESERVOIR: Large shoals of big Bream have appeared here in recent years. Recommended fishing areas include the small bay at Oak Grove, down from the bad bend beyond Carrigadrohid village approximately 500 yards below Dripsey Bridge and below the boating centre just above Inniscarra Dam. Good stocks of Pike, Rudd, Perch and Eels are also present.

For a detailed Lee System brochure, contact the SWRFB (026) 41221.

CORK CITY

THE LOUGH: This 10 acre lake lies within Cork City. It is Ireland's only big Carp water and holds the Irish Record Carp of 26 lbs 2 oz which was recorded 28 May 1989. This open water is accessible for disabled anglers. It also holds a big stock of small Rudd, Perch and Tench and Eels to specimen size.

The Lough is also a Wildfowl Sanctuary and anglers must take care not to leave line or hooks around.

BALLINCOLLIG RESERVOIR: This is an old disused reservoir 3 miles south of Ballincollig west of Cork City. It holds good stocks of Carp and some Tench.

ANGLING CONTACT

Noel Hackett, South Western Regional Fisheries Board, Macroom, Tel (026) 41221.

MALLOW

Mallow, in north Co. Cork, is on the River Blackwater up-river from Fermoy on the N72. The fast-moving river has mixed fishing and its waters are controlled by local clubs with some private stretches. Roach and Dace feed here throughout the year, but catches are best during the colder months. Fishing here is in the River Blackwater only.

CLUB

Mallow AC, Dick Willis, Bridge House Bar, Mallow, Tel (022) 21057.

ANGLING CONTACTS

Dick Willis, Bridge House Bar.
The local hotel and guesthouse owners are experienced in dealing with anglers.

TACKLE SHOPS

Mallow Sports Centre, 21 Bridge Street, Mallow.

BAIT

Jack O'Sullivan, 4 Patrick Street, Fermoy, Tel (025) 31110.

SPECIES

Roach, Dace, Perch, Pike, Eels.

■ MALLOW

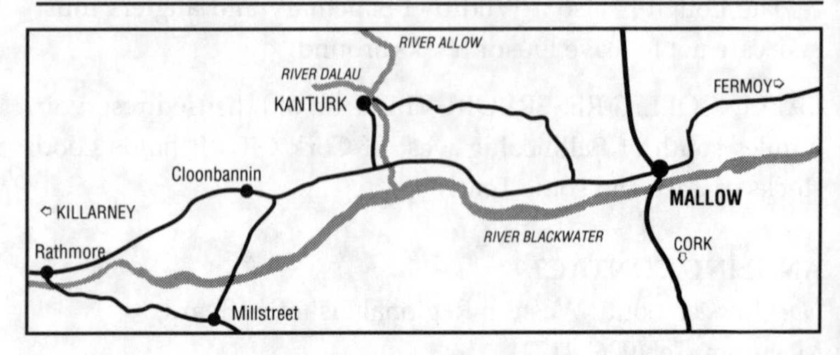

RIVER BLACKWATER: The river in this area has both fast and slow-making stretches and is liable to flood after heavy rain. In the town at the Creamery Stretch, the park and below the bridge, Roach and Dace provide good sport. Farther downriver at the coursing field, there are also good Roach and Dace.

Special Note: The River Blackwater is a mixed fishery and anglers must acquaint themselves with local regulations and seek permission to fish some stretches.

County Donegal

BALLYSHANNON

Ballyshannon is situated on the Donegal-Sligo road (N15) straddling the River Erne just before it enters the sea. This busy Co. Donegal town is dominated by a hydro-electric station above the bridge. Fishing for coarse fish is in the big reservoir, which is called Assaroe Lake, and some other smaller lakes to the north. Roach are common in Assaroe, with some Bream, Hybrids, Perch, Pike, and Eels. Roach are at their best in the colder months. Fishing in this area is in lakes.

ANGLING CONTACTS

Northern Regional Fisheries Board, Station Road, Ballyshannon.
ESB, Tel (072) 51435.

TACKLE SHOPS

Pat Barrett's, Main Street, Bundoran.
Jack Philips, West End, Bundoran.
Ms E. McAloon, Newsagent, Ballyshannon.

BAIT

Irish Angling Services, Ardlougher, Ballyconnell, Tel (049) 26258.

SPECIES

Bream, Roach, Perch, Pike, Eels.

BALLYSHANNON

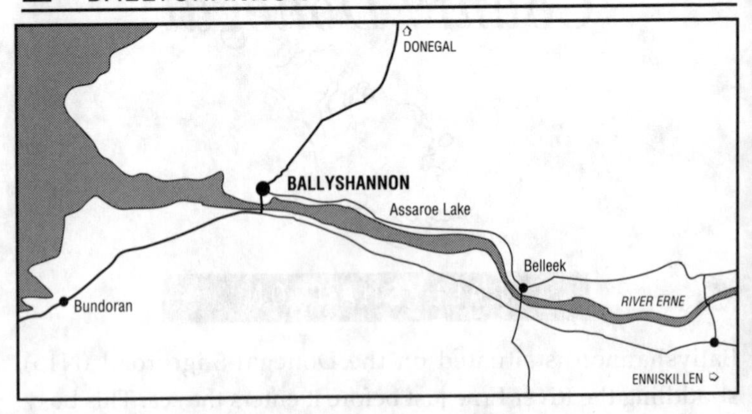

ASSAROE LAKE: This big reservoir above the hydro-electric station is a mixed fishery.

The lake is accessible along its northern side, where there are entry points to the main lake to the south and a smaller section to the north of the road. Fishing is also available at some points on the southern side off the Ballyshannon-Belleek road. This lake holds a substantial stock of good Roach, with some Bream, Hybrids, Perch, Pike and Eels.

This man-made water has many submerged hazards and is liable to water fluctuations.

Special Notice: This water is controlled by the ESB and all regulations must be adhered to. Permits to fish Assaroe Lake cost £5.00 per year (£2.00 for two weeks) and can be obtained from the ESB Office, Ballyshannon.

Permission must also be obtained to put a boat on this lake. There are special regulations for boat-users.

North of Ballyshannon, there are some lakes east of the Ballyshannon-Donegal road. These waters hold some Perch, Pike and Eels.

County Dublin

DUBLIN

DUBLIN

In Dublin city, there are the Grand and Royal Canals with stocks of coarse fish. There is also the River Liffey which holds some coarse fish in sections. There is also some good coarse fishing on the reservoir on the River Liffey.

CLUB

Dublin Coarse Fishing Angling Club, Alan Larkin, 72 Dargle Wood, Templeogue, Dublin, Tel (01) 946454.

ANGLING CONTACTS

Tackle dealers in Dublin will advise on waters.

Eastern Regional Fisheries Board, Glasnevin, Dublin.

TACKLE SHOPS

Rory's Fishing Tackle, 17a Temple Bar, Dublin 2, Tel (01) 772351.

Gaynestown Ltd, May Mel, Main Street, Blanchardstown, Dublin 15, Tel (01) 201127.

Tallaght Gun Shop, Castletymon Shopping Centre, Tallaght, Dublin 24, Tel (01) 526522.

DAP Sports, Derravaragh, Clondalkin, Dublin 22, Tel (01) 280546.

BAIT

Rory's Fishing Tackle, 17a Temple Bar, Dublin 2, Tel (01) 772351.

WATERS FISHED

Canal, river, lake.

OTHER WATERS IN THIS AREA

See Prosperous.

SPECIES

Roach, Bream, Hybrids, Perch, Tench, Pike, Rudd, Eels.

MAPS

Central Fisheries Board Angling Map – Prosperous.

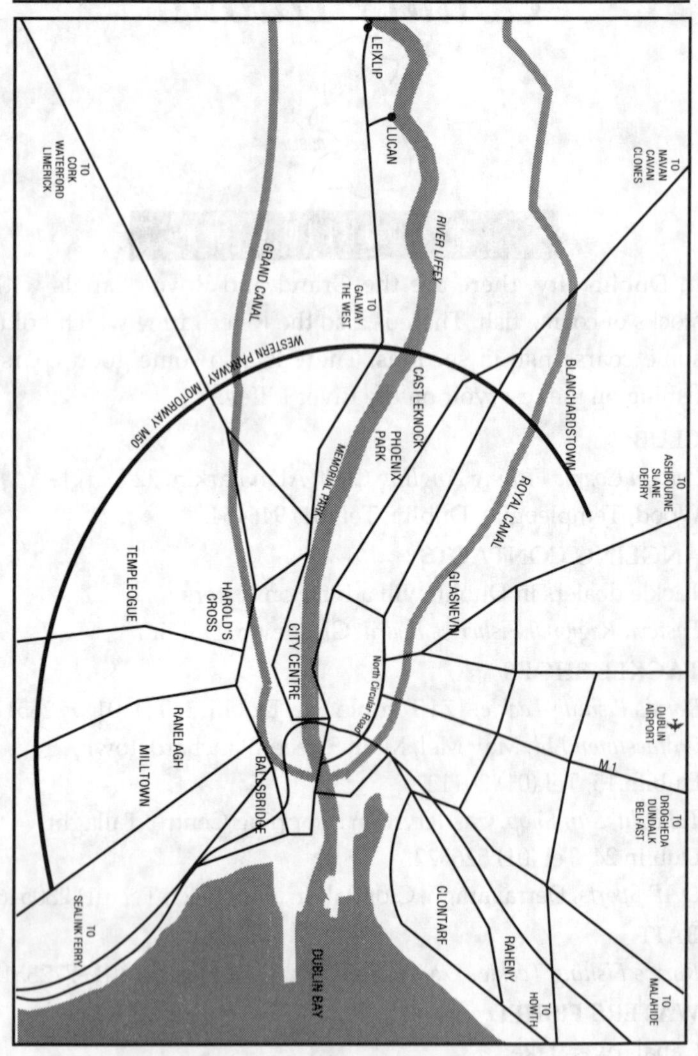

RIVER LIFFEY: The Liffey flows through Leixlip reservoir, on through Lucan and enters Dublin at the Memorial Park in Islandbridge.

Special Note: The Liffey is a mixed fishery with Salmon and Trout. Most of its waters are in private ownership. Coarse fish anglers should note those stretches, observe all club regulations and have permission to fish.

LEIXLIP RESERVOIR: This water above the Leixlip dam is leased by the Dublin Trout Anglers. Roach, Rudd, good quality Rudd/Bream Hybrids, Perch, Pike and some Tench provide good sport here. Access is by the gate beside the Salmon Leap Inn and then over private property to the water.
Note: This is a densely populated part of the city. Problems of safe parking etc. may arise.
CPI FACTORY, LUCAN: Entry to the river here is at the private CPI factory car park. This stretch is controlled by the Dublin Salmon Anglers. There is an abundance of small Roach, with Rudd, Hybrids, Perch and Pike.
Note: This is a densely populated part of the city where problems of safe parking may exist.
MEMORIAL PARK: The fishing is opposite the rowing club at Islandbridge. There is some Roach fishing here in the summer. There is also a fair stock of Hybrids, Perch and Pike here.
GRAND CANAL: The canal from Dublin connects with the River Shannon at Shannon harbour.

Within Dublin city, there is some good coarse fishing. The stretch near Dolphin's Barn holds good stocks of Roach, Bream, Hybrids, Perch, some Pike, Tench and Eels.

Locks 1–3 Suir Road Bridge to Naas Road (main line): There is good sport here for Roach, Rudd, Hybrids, Perch, Pike and Eels. Near Clondalkin, there are some Tench. Below Lucan Road Bridge there is a big stock of small Tench.
ROYAL CANAL: This canal runs from Dublin to Mullingar, where it is now dewatered west of the town.

The first fishing in Dublin is between Locks 1–5 where there are some Roach, Roach/Bream Hybrids, Perch, Pike and Eels. Then between Lock 6 and 7 at Shandon Mills, there is good sport for Roach, Roach/Bream Hybrids, Perch, Eels. Above Reilly's Bridge, the stretch is good for Roach and Hybrids, with some Tench. Above Lock 12, although weedy at times, it provides good fishing for Roach, with some Tench. Near Lucan, above Lock 12, there is also a good stretch for Roach, Rudd, Hybrids, Perch and Eels.

County Galway

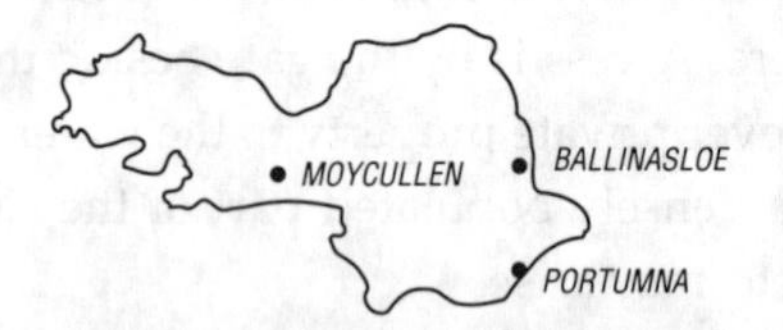

BALLINASLOE

Ballinasloe, on the River Suck, is located on the Dublin/Galway road (N6) 100 miles (160 km) west of Dublin. This is a busy market town situated in low-lying countryside. The town has all facilities for sport and relaxation, including golf club and tennis courts etc.

Bream and Rudd come on here from April to October, with quality Bream showing in the middle summer months. Tench fishing is best in May and June. Pike fishing is good all year, but the most productive time is in the winter months. Roach stocks are small at this time, but they will increase in numbers in the coming years. Fishing in this area is mostly in the River Suck.

CLUB

Ballinasloe Gala Angling Club, Pat Lawless, 4 Hillcrest Park, Ballinasloe.

ANGLING CONTACTS

Tony Ellis, Square D Factory; also 2 Ard Mhuire, Ballinasloe, Tel (0905) 42668.

Hotel and guesthouse owners are experienced in dealing with anglers.

TACKLE SHOPS

L. Keller, Main Street, Ballinasloe.

Salmon's, Main Street, Ballinasloe.

Killeen's Shop, Shannonbridge.

BAIT

D. Killeen, Shannonbridge, Tel (0905) 74112.
Bill Burton, 'Woodlands', Dublin Road, Ballinasloe, Tel (0905) 43123.

OTHER WATERS IN THIS AREA

See Athlone, Shannonbridge, Banagher, Portumna, Castlecoote.

SPECIES

Bream, Rudd, Hybrids, Perch, Tench, Eels and Roach.

COMPETITIONS

Ballinasloe Gala Week – May.

BALLINASLOE

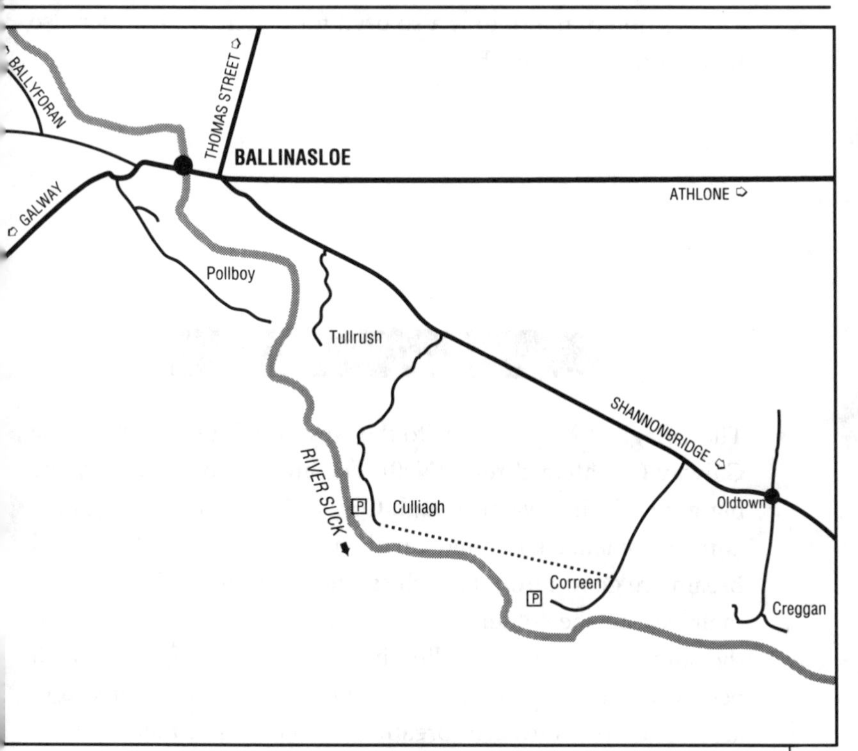

RIVER SUCK: The river up from Ballinasloe to the Derrycahill Stretch near Ballyforan has many good sections scattered through the low-lying countryside.

At Derrycahill, in the bog, the banks are open and fishing is for Bream, Rudd, Perch and Pike. Near Ahascragh, at Daly's Grove, there is a good Bream stretch. The river below Ballinasloe has a short stretch with quality Bream, but it is at Culliagh where the river is at its best for Bream, Rudd and Perch with some Roach. This is a match stretch with clean banks and soft margins in places. The area is liable to flood.

At Correen Ford, there is a deep pool which holds Bream, Rudd and some Roach. From there downriver, by Creggan to the confluence with the River Shannon at Shannonbridge, there are shoals of Bream and Rudd, with Perch, Pike and Roach. This section of the river is also used for matches. The river also holds some good Tench.

MOYCULLEN

The village of Moycullen is to the west of Lough Corrib on the Galway-Oughterard road (N59). The area is dominated by the big game fishing water, Lough Corrib. The coarse fishing here is in the smaller lakes and canals near the village. Roach and Bream are good throughout the summer, with quality Roach at their best in the colder months. Rudd and Tench feed best in the summer, and Pike angling in the rich waters is good, with best results usually attained in winter. Fishing in this area is in lakes and rivers. Roach/Bream hybrids of specimen size are also found in this area.

CLUB

Galway Coarse Angling Club, Hugh Kearns, Finny PO, Clonbur, Tel (091) 85566.

ANGLING CONTACTS

Danny Goldrick, Western Regional Fisheries Board, Tel (091) 63118.

TACKLE SHOPS

Hugh Duffy, Mainguard Street, Galway.
Freeney's, High Street, Galway.
Great Outdoors, Eglinton Street, Galway.

BAIT

Hugh Duffy, Mainguard Street, Galway, Tel (091) 62367
Tommy Kavanagh, Cloonabinnia Hotel, Moycullen, Tel (091) 85555/85512.

OTHER WATERS IN THIS AREA

See Ballinasloe.

SPECIES

Bream, Roach, Rudd, Hybrid, Pike, Eels, Tench.

1. BALLYQUIRKE LAKE: This 150 acre water, the bigger of the Moycullen lakes, is beside the main Galway road and is connected to Lough Corrib by a canal. A rich water, it holds good stocks of Bream to 8 lbs (3.6 kg), with good Roach, Rudd, Hybrids, Perch, Pike, and Eels. Parking is beside the lake and fishing is from a good bank. Suitable for disabled anglers. There are access points to this well developed fishery.
2. LOUGH DOWN: This is really two lakes connected by a slow-moving stream. The smaller lake has soft, reeded shores. The bigger lake too has soft margins and fishing is from stands into about 20 feet of water. This is a good water for good-sized Bream, with Roach, Hybrids, Perch, Rudd, Tench and Pike.

   These waters are within a forest and anglers should respect the property of the state forestry – Coillte Teoranta. Access road is near Moycullen Church.

MOYCULLEN

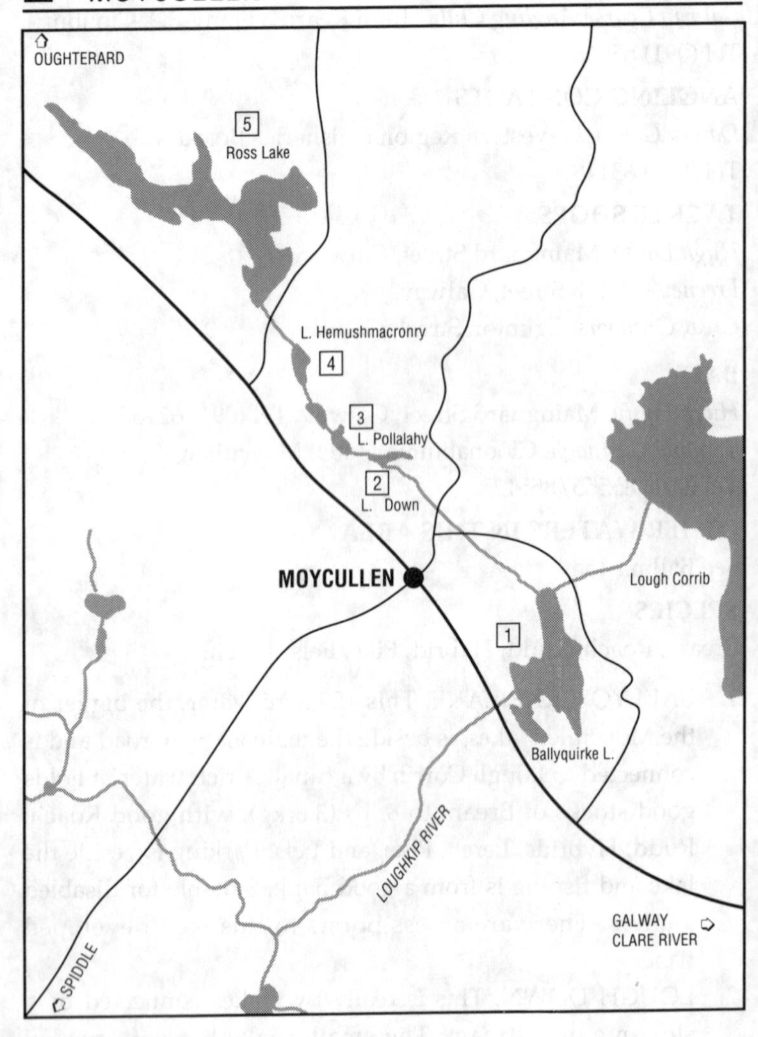
OUGHTERARD
5
Ross Lake
L. Hemushmacronry
4
3
L. Pollalahy
2
L. Down
MOYCULLEN
Lough Corrib
1
Ballyquirke L.
LOUGHKIP RIVER
GALWAY
CLARE RIVER
SPIDDLE

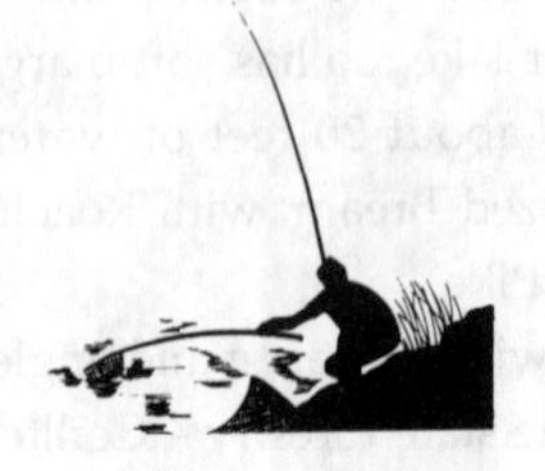

3. LOUGH POLLALAHY: This lake is fishable along its northern bank and holds a stock of Roach, some Bream, Rudd, Perch, Pike and Eels. This water is approached from Lough Down.
4. HEMUSHMACRONRY LAKE: The access to this 20-acre lake is off the Lallinamuct Road. The water is well developed and fishing is into 12 feet of water for good Bream, Fench, Roach and Hybrids.
5. ROSS LAKE: This is a 400-acre lake with access at three places. There is car parking along the southern shore where fishing from stands is into about 15 feet. There are also some swims near the Cloonabinnia Hotel. The Annagh Wood section has also good fishing in 12 feet of water.

   This excellent lake holds good stocks of quality Roach, Bream and Hybrids. Tench are found near the outflow where there is more weed.

CLARE RIVER: This river flowing into Lough Corrib is crossed by the Headfort/Galway road bridge. Access is best along the west bank where there is first-class fishing for good Roach and Hybrids.

CORRIB RIVER, GALWAY: The new by-pass bridge has some access to this river which flows through the city. Here in the warmer months, there is good Roach and Hybrid fishing.

BALLINDOOLEY PONDS: North-east of Galway and off the N84 road at one mile, there are two ponds which have shallow, soft, weedy surrounds. There are some Tench to 6 lbs, with Rudd and Perch.

PARKYFAHERTY LAKE: This 15-acre lake is well developed and is north of Moycullen. The access is easy and there is fishing into varying depths to 15 feet. The water produces Bream, Roach, Hybrids and Rudd.

PORTUMNA

Portumna, on the west bank of the River Shannon, is located about midway on the Nenagh-Loughrea road. A town beside the River Shannon, it has a busy boating marina at the top of Lough Derg. Bream come on the feed from May to October, and Rudd give good sport over the summer months. Tench are at their best in May and June. Pike fishing is good all year, but the winter sport is best. Fishing here is in the River Shannon, Lough Derg and one small lake.

CLUB

Portumna Development Co., Owen O'Carroll, Portland, Nr Lorrha, Tel (0509) 47143.

ANGLING CONTACTS

Owen O'Carroll, Portumna, Tel (0509) 47143.

Hotel and guesthouse owners are experienced in dealing with anglers.

TACKLE SHOP

Garry Kenny's Shop, Palmerstown.

BAIT

Owen O'Carroll, Portland, Nr Lorrha, Tel (0509) 47143.

Bertie Cummins, Meelick, Tel (0905) 75202.

OTHER WATERS IN THIS AREA

See Banagher, Ballinasloe, O'Brien's Bridge, Tulla.

SPECIES

Bream, Rudd, Hybrids, Perch, Pike, Tench, Eels.

BOATS

Owen O'Carroll, Portland, Nr Lorrha. Tel (0509) 47143.

PORTUMNA

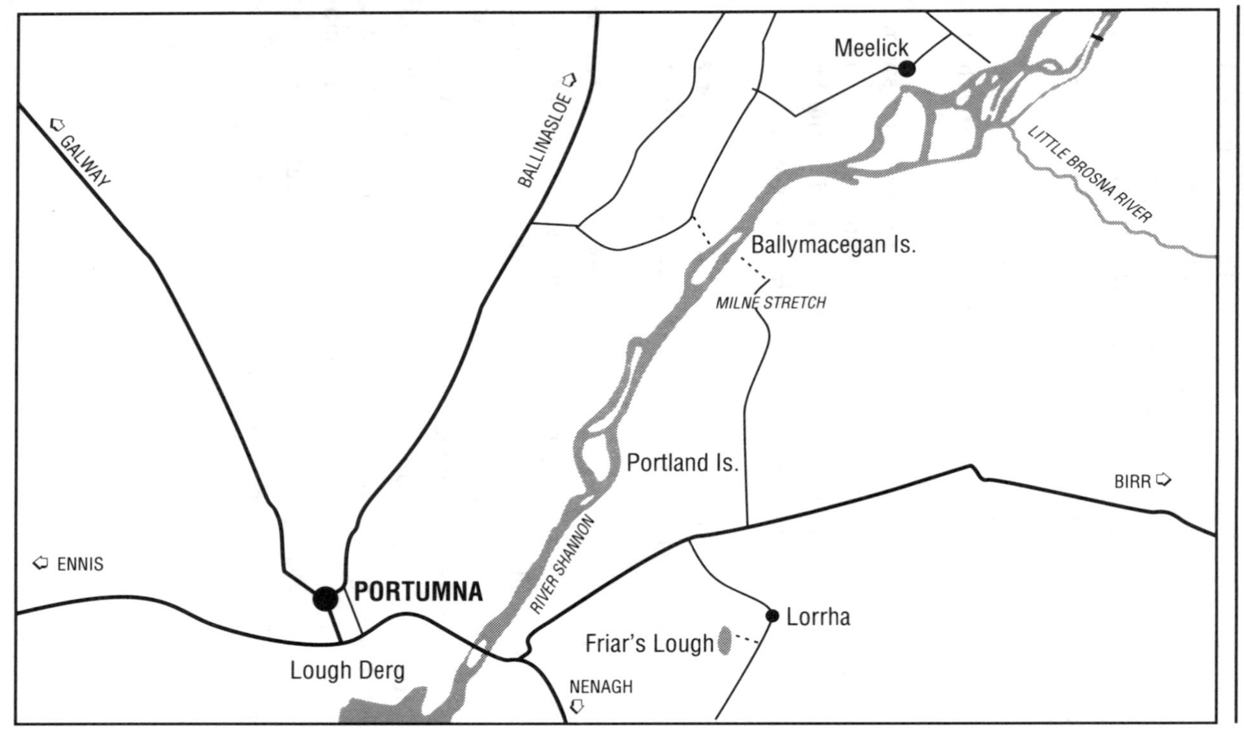
Meelick
LITTLE BROSNA RIVER
Ballymacegan Is.
MILNE STRETCH
GALWAY
BALLINASLOE
Portland Is.
BIRR
RIVER SHANNON
ENNIS
PORTUMNA
Lorrha
Friar's Lough
Lough Derg
NENAGH

RIVER SHANNON: The river at Meelick has a weir and lock. The waters here are rich, with good Rudd, Bream, Hybrids, Perch and Pike. From this point down to Portumna, there are many areas of excellent fishing, mostly approached from a boat. There is first-class bank fishing on the wide river, approached off the Ballinasloe road to a quiet backwater behind Ballymacegan Island.

There are great stocks of Bream here. On the east bank of the Shannon on the Tipperary side, the Milne stretch also produces good Bream and Rudd fishing.

Above the bridge at Portumna, there are many swims, developed by the Fisheries Board, which produce good Bream, Rudd and Hybrids. On the tip of the island at the bridge, Bream and Rudd fishing are good during the summer.

FRIAR'S LOUGH: Near Lorrha, this small lake holds Bream to 4 lbs (1.8 kg), with Perch, Rudd, Pike, Eels, and some Tench.

LOUGH DERG: This is a big, open water with good stocks of Pike, Rudd, Hybrids, Tench, Perch, Eels, some Roach and also Brown Trout. Perch are common all over and can be found near harbours. Bream are located at many places but it is essential to bait heavily for these fish. At Lough Derg Caravan Park, there is good Bream fishing, especially in the early and late hours. Church Bay holds great stocks of Tench and Rudd. The Scarriff River is also a fine fishery with good Bream and Perch and also Rudd and Pike. The reeded areas around the many islands in this big lake offer great opportunities to explore and have good fishing.

County Kildare

ATHY

Athy, on the River Barrow, is situated about 12 miles (10 km) north of Carlow on the Dublin-Kilkenny road. It is south of Monasterevan and Vicarstown. The Barrow branch of the Grand Canal joins the river at the town. Bream feed mid April to October and Rudd give good sport during summer months. Tench in the canal also provide good sport in the summer. Pike fishing in the river is good throughout the year, with the best fishing coming during the colder months. There are some good Perch in the river.

CLUBS

Monasterevan Anglers Club, James Rosney, Cowpasture, Monasterevan.
Vicarstown Anglers, James Crean, Vicarstown, Co. Laois, Tel (0502) 25189.
Kilberry and Cloney Anglers Association, Larry Foy, Kilberry, Co. Kildare.
Athy and District AC, Brendan Murphy (Publican), Main Street, Athy.

ANGLING CONTACTS All clubs will assist anglers. Guesthouse owners are experienced in dealing with anglers.

TACKLE SHOPS

Griffin Hawe Ltd, 22 Duke Street, Athy, Tel (0507) 31575/31221.
J. Boyd, Motor and Sports, Tully Street, Carlow.

BAIT

Griffin Hawe, 22 Duke Street, Athy, Tel (0507) 31575/31221.

J. Crean, Vicarstown Inn, Vicarstown, Tel (0502) 25189.

OTHER WATERS IN THIS AREA

See Carlow, Prosperous, Durrow/Ballinakill.

SPECIES

Bream, Rudd, Hybrids, Tench, Perch, Pike, Eels.

ATHY

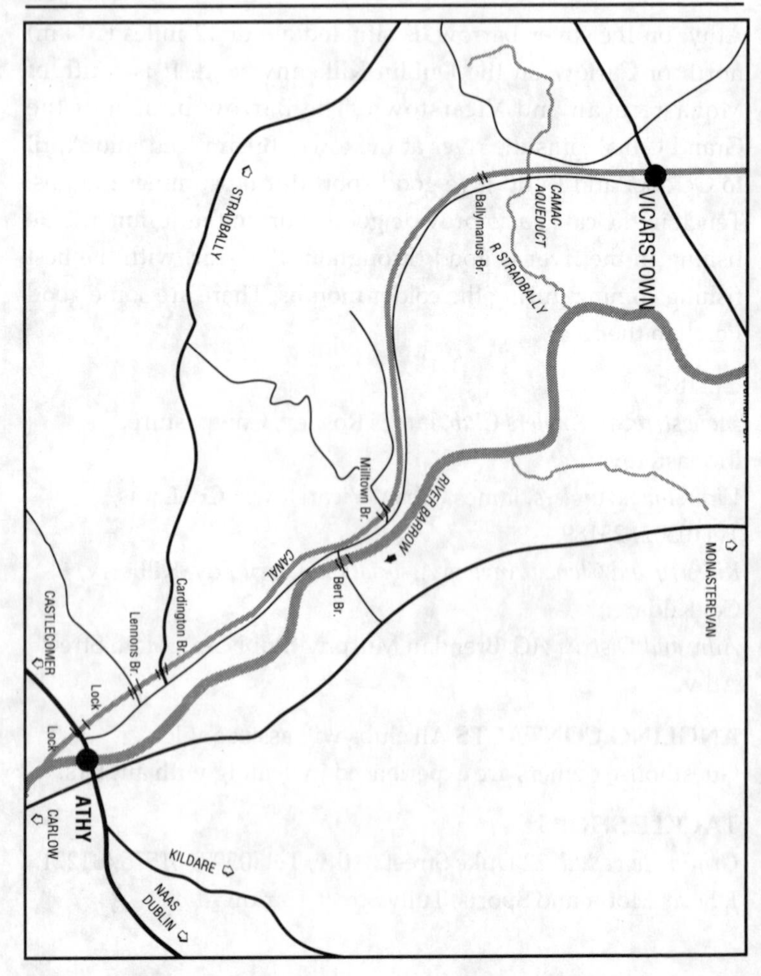

RIVER BARROW: The River Barrow rises in the Slieve Bloom Mountains and from Monasterevan flows directly south. It is a big river, draining a large area, and after heavy rain it can flood quickly. The flow is moderate to fast in places.

From Monasterevan, the river is excellent for coarse fish. Anglers will find some shoals of good-quality Perch. The river is weedy and has some deep holes which hold good stocks of Bream and Rudd. Rudd fishing is particularly good around Dunrally Bridge. The shallow waters upriver of Athy hold Bream, Rudd and an abundance of Perch. Between the town bridge in Athy and Ardleigh Lock, large shoals of big Bream congregate in May/June, when catches of over 100 lbs (45 kg) are taken.

BARROW CANAL: The Barrow branch of the Grand Canal runs parallel to the River Barrow and provides good sport. The canal beside the angling centre of Vicarstown has Bream and Rudd. Further down towards Athy, there are some Tench to 6 lbs (2.7 kg). The canal joins with the River Barrow in Athy town.

Special note: The River Barrow is a mixed fishery with Salmon and Trout. Anglers should note the game fishing stretches and observe local club regulations.

PROSPEROUS

Prosperous is situated on the Dublin-Edenderry Road (R403) about 20 miles (32 km) to the west of Dublin. The village is located on the northern side of the Grand Canal. Tench fishing is good from late April to July. Bream fishing is best from mid-April to October. Rudd feed in the summer months. Perch and some Pike provide sport throughout the year. Fishing here is on the Grand Canal.

CLUB

Prosperous Coarse Angling Club, Ned O'Farrell, Curryhills, Prosperous, Tel (045) 68092.

ANGLING CONTACTS

Ned O'Farrell, Curryhills, Prosperous.
Guesthouse owners are experienced in dealing with anglers.

BAIT

Countryman Angling, Pacelli Road, Naas, Tel (045) 79341.

OTHER WATERS IN THIS AREA

See Enfield, Athy, Carlow.

SPECIES

Bream, Rudd, Tench, Perch, Pike, Eels.

COMPETITION

Prosperous Angling Festival in May.

GRAND CANAL: The stretch from Digby bridge to above Landenstown bridge is a first-class fishery. There are good Tench here to 6 lbs (2.7 kg), with Rudd, Hybrids, some Bream, Perch, Pike and Eels. Above the bridge, there are some Bream and Rudd to Robertstown. From Shee bridge to Ticknevin, there is some very good fishing for Bream, with Rudd, Perch, Eels and some Pike. Farther along, at Edenderry, the canal provides good fishing for Bream, with Rudd and Perch.

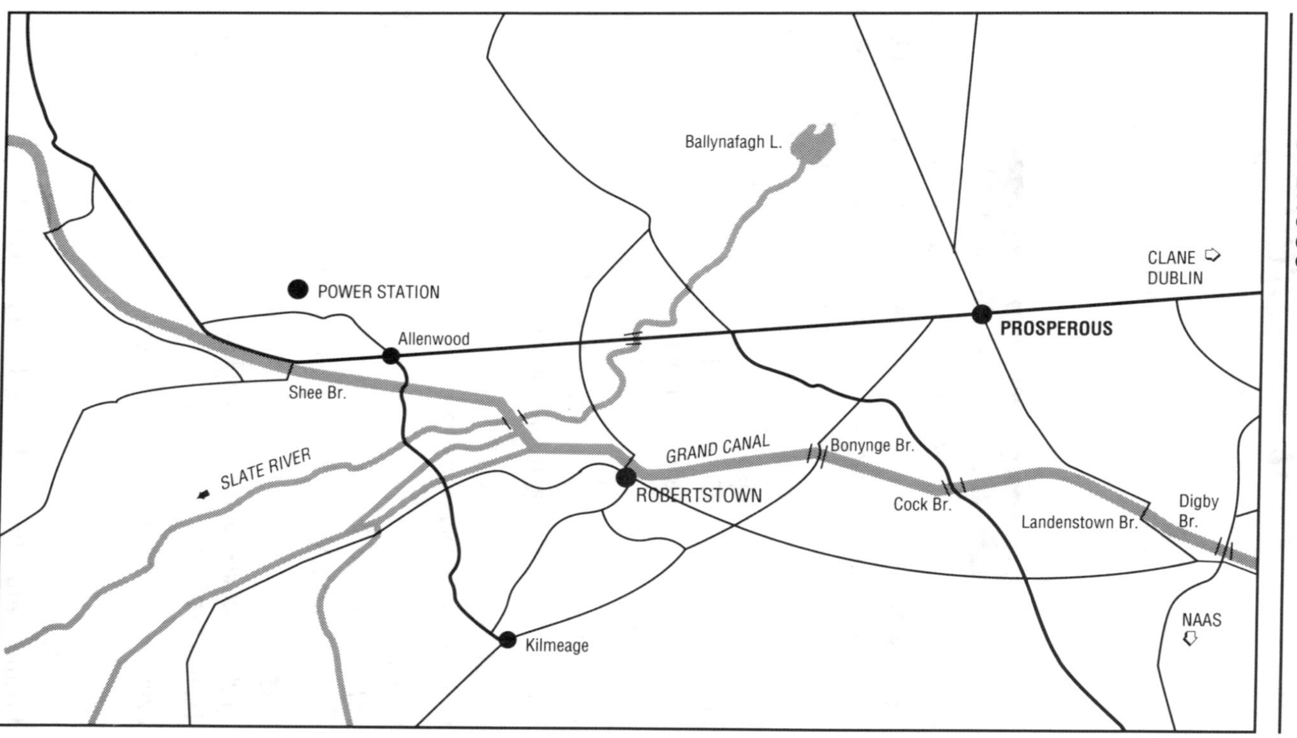
Ballynafagh L.
CLANE
DUBLIN
POWER STATION
PROSPEROUS
Allenwood
Shee Br.
GRAND CANAL
Bonynge Br.
SLATE RIVER
ROBERTSTOWN
Cock Br.
Digby
Br.
Landenstown Br.
NAAS
Kilmeage

County Kilkenny

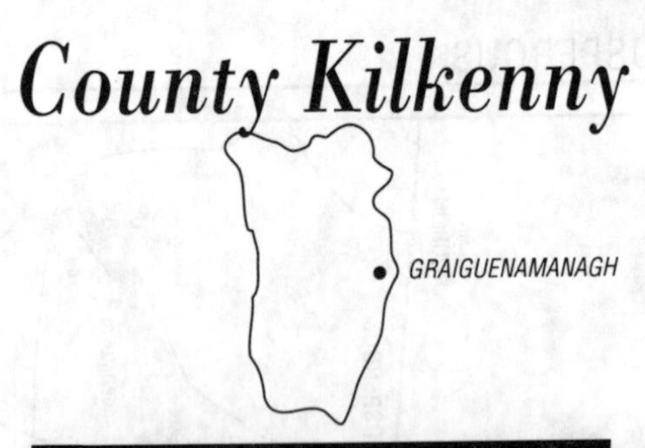

GRAIGUENAMANAGH

Graiguenamanagh is situated in the Barrow Valley on the Carlow-New Ross road, 74 miles (120 km) from Dublin. Graiguenamanagh is along the west side of the River Barrow in scenic countryside. Bream fishing is good from May to late September, while Rudd give excellent sport in summer. Perch and Pike fishing is also good in summer, but the best Pike are taken in the winter. Tench feed freely in May and June. Fishing in this area is on the River Barrow.

CLUB

Barrow Valley Tourist Association, Mrs Alice McCabe, Brandon View House, Ballyogan, Graiguenamanagh, Tel (0503) 24191.

ANGLING CONTACTS

Guesthouse owners are experienced in dealing with anglers.

TACKLE SHOPS

O'Leary's Tackle Shop, Main Street, Graiguenamanagh.
M. McCullagh, Market Square, Bagnalstown, Tel (0503) 21381.

BAIT

Michael McCabe, Brandon View House, Ballyogan, Graig, Tel (0503) 24191.

OTHER WATERS IN THIS AREA

See Athy, Carlow.

SPECIES

Bream, Rudd, Hybrids, Perch, Tench, Pike, Eels.

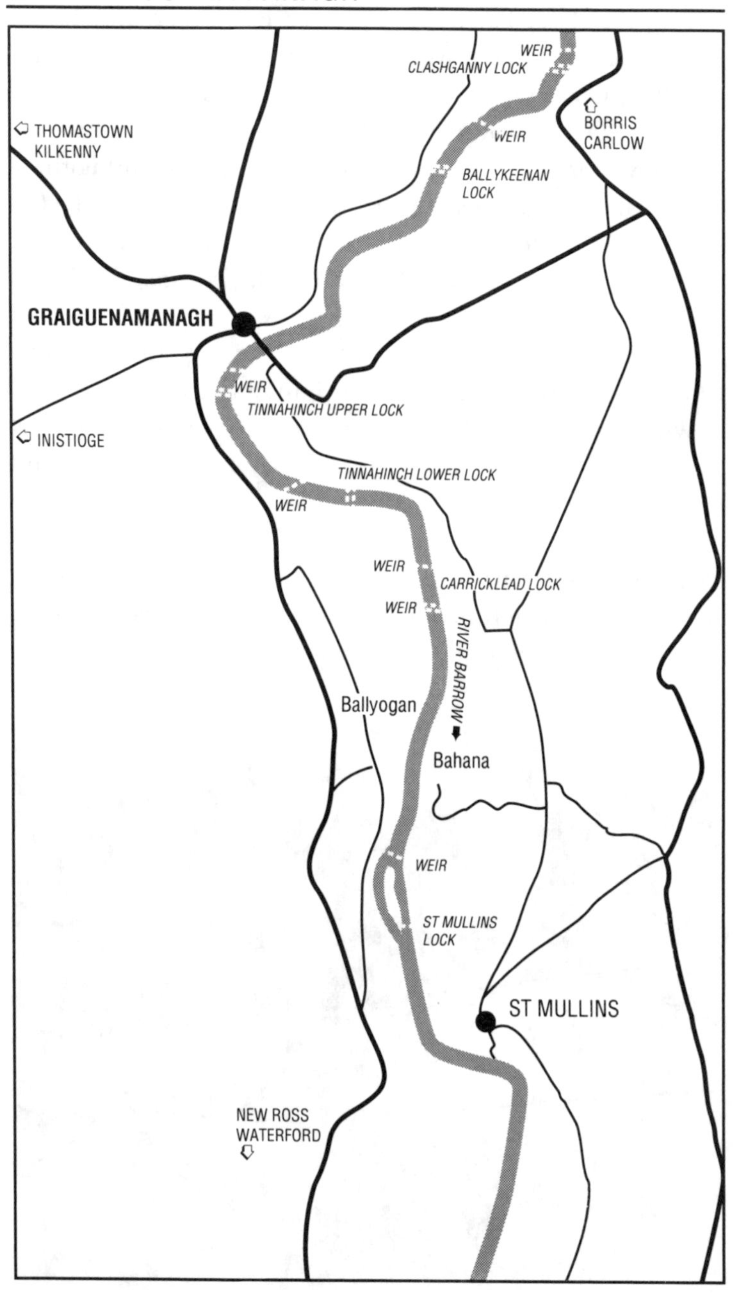
WEIR
CLASHGANNY LOCK
THOMASTOWN
KILKENNY
BORRIS
CARLOW
WEIR
BALLYKEENAN
LOCK
GRAIGUENAMANAGH
WEIR
TINNAHINCH UPPER LOCK
INISTIOGE
TINNAHINCH LOWER LOCK
WEIR
WEIR
CARRICKLEAD LOCK
WEIR
RIVER BARROW
Ballyogan
Bahana
WEIR
ST MULLINS
LOCK
ST MULLINS
NEW ROSS
WATERFORD

RIVER BARROW: Flowing through a picturesque and fertile valley, the River Barrow in this area has a moderate-to-fast flow. There are several weirs and locks, with short, quiet canal stretches. Good Pike are found from Bagnalstown all the way down to the tidal waters at St Mullins.

Below Borris at Clashganny weir, 3 miles (4.8 km) north of Graiguenamanagh, there is good Bream fishing just at the fast water. 400 m downriver there is a first-class stretch for specimen fish, i.e. Bream, Tench, Rudd, Hybrids, Perch and Pike.

At Tinnahinch in the town, there is a big stock of small Rudd and Perch. From here to Bahana, 2 miles (3.2 km) downriver, the river holds Bream to 7 lbs (3 kg). The quiet canal waters always hold Rudd, with some Tench. Good fishing is to be had at the St Mullin's lock canal section.

Note: The River Barrow is a mixed fishery and holds Trout, Salmon and coarse fish. Anglers should note the game fishing stretches and observe all local club regulations.

County Laois

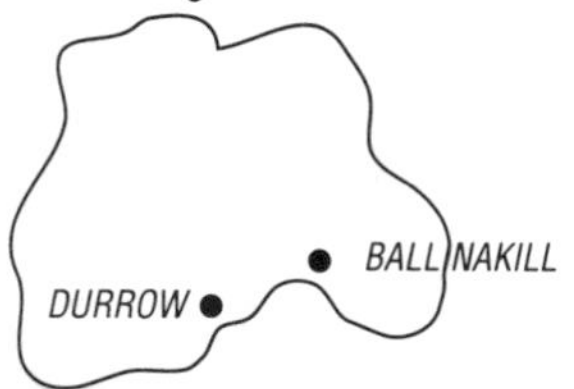

DURROW – BALLINAKILL

Durrow is a small town on the Portlaoise-Cork road (N8), about 15 miles (24 km) south of Portlaoise. The village of Ballinakill is just to the east. In this area, there are some interesting small waters.

Tench are at their best in the early summer but will feed into the cold months. Rudd and Perch also provide good summer sport here.

CLUB

Durrow and Cullowhill Angling Club. Michael Walsh, 18 Erkindale Drive, Durrow.

ANGLING CONTACTS

Bill Lawlor, Newsagent/Tackle Shop, Durrow.

TACKLE SHOP

Bill Lawlor, Durrow, Tel (0502) 36234

BAIT

Bill Lawlor, Durrow, Tel (0502) 36234

SPECIES

Rudd, Tench, Perch Pike, Eels.

1. GRANTSTOWN LAKE: Situated in a forest west of Durrow, this lovely water offers good sport for quality Tench. A weeded sheltered water, it fishes best in May-June, after which the Tench can be taken more slowly through to October. This good water also holds quality Rudd, some good-quality Perch, Pike and Eels.

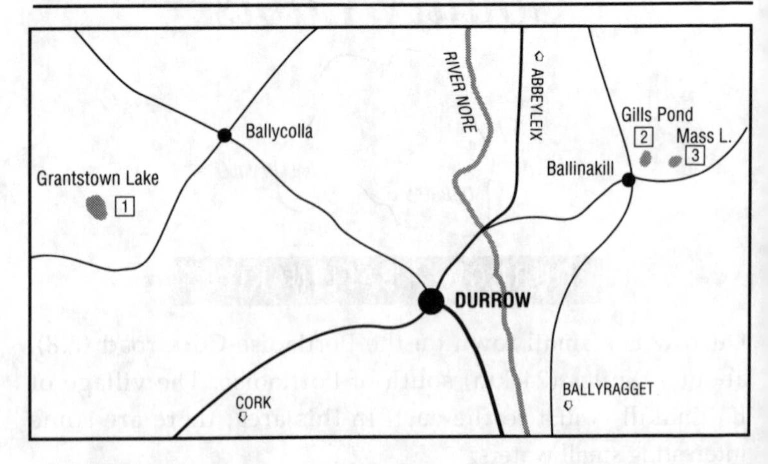

Grantstown Lake is within the property of Coillte Teo and landowners' property must be respected. Fishing is restricted to members of the Durrow and Ballinakill AC. Permits are obtainable from Bill Lawlor, Newsagent Shop, Durrow.

2. GILLS POND: This is a small pond beside Ballinakill and near the Salesian Brothers School. A very weedy water, it holds some Tench, Rudd and Perch.
3. MASS LOUGH: Near Gills Pond, Mass Lough is beside the road and has easy access. This water has weedy patches and holds good Tench to 4 lbs (1.8 kg). It also holds small Rudd, Perch and small Pike.

ERKING RIVER: This water west of Durrow produces Pike in the winter/spring months.

County Leitrim

BALLINAMORE

Ballinamore is situated on the Cavan-Carrick on Shannon road about 20 miles (32 km) to the west of Cavan. Ballinamore is a busy town located in the western arm of the River Erne system. Bream fishing is good from mid April to October. Roach, Perch and Pike provide sport throughout the year, but it is during the colder months that the big Pike are best. Tench fishing is good in May/June but continues into September. Fishing here is in a variety of lakes and a river.

CLUBS

Ballinamore Tourist Development Association, Maura Sweeney, Woodview, Aghadark, Ballinamore, Tel (078) 44434.

ANGLING CONTACTS

Guesthouse owners in this area are experienced in dealing with anglers.

TACKLE SHOPS

Mrs Elderton, Newsagent, Main Street, Ballinamore, Tel (078) 44080.

BAIT

Mrs Elderton, Newsagent, Main Street, Ballinamore, Tel (078) 44080.

OTHER WATERS IN THIS AREA

See Ballyconnell, Killeshandra, Carrigallen, Mohill, Drumshanbo, Carrick-on-Shannon.

SPECIES

Bream, Roach, Rudd, Hybrids, Tench, Perch, Pike, Eels.

BOATS

Brian Kennedy, Aughoo, Ballinamore.

Ivan Price, Ardrum, Ballinamore, Tel (078) 44278.

John O'Donoghue, Keshcarrigan, Ballinamore, Tel (078) 42002.

Michael Flanagan, Drumreilly, Garadice, Tel (049) 33382.

1. BOLGANARD LAKE: Off the Cavan road, this reeded lake holds Roach, Bream, Perch, Pike, Eels and Tench.
2. CORGAR LAKE: This lake is good for specimen Tench in May and June. It also has Roach, Rudd, Hybrids, Perch, Pike and Eels. This lake is beside Bolganard.
3. DRUMLONAN LAKE: A shallow water which is fished from stands. It holds quality Tench, Rudd, Roach, Hybrids, Perch, Pike and Eels. This lake is an extension of Corgar Lake.
4. CORDUFF LAKE: This water is beside the Bawnboy road and has a good stock of Tench to 4 lbs (1.8 kg), with Roach, Perch, Pike, Eels and some Bream.
5. GARADICE LAKE: This is a very big lake along the Killeshandra road, with many good fishing stretches which have easy access and good parking. Bream and Roach abound in most places, with Hybrids, Perch, Pike and Eels. The sections which have all facilities are Houghton's Shore (suitable for disabled anglers), Church and Connolly's Shore. The outflow at Houghton's goes into Little Garadice which is worth a try for Roach and Bream.
6. DRUMCOURA LAKE: This is a shallow lake which produces good fishing. It has an excellent stock of Bream to 6 lbs (2.7 kg), with Roach, Rudd, Hybrids, Perch, Pike and Eels. The water can be approached off the Carrigallen road and parking is easy.
7. KEENKEEN LAKE: The stock of Bream in this lake near the Carrigallen road is limited to a few shoals of good-quality fish to 6 lbs (2.7 kg). It also has some good Roach, Hybrids, Perch, Pike and Eels.

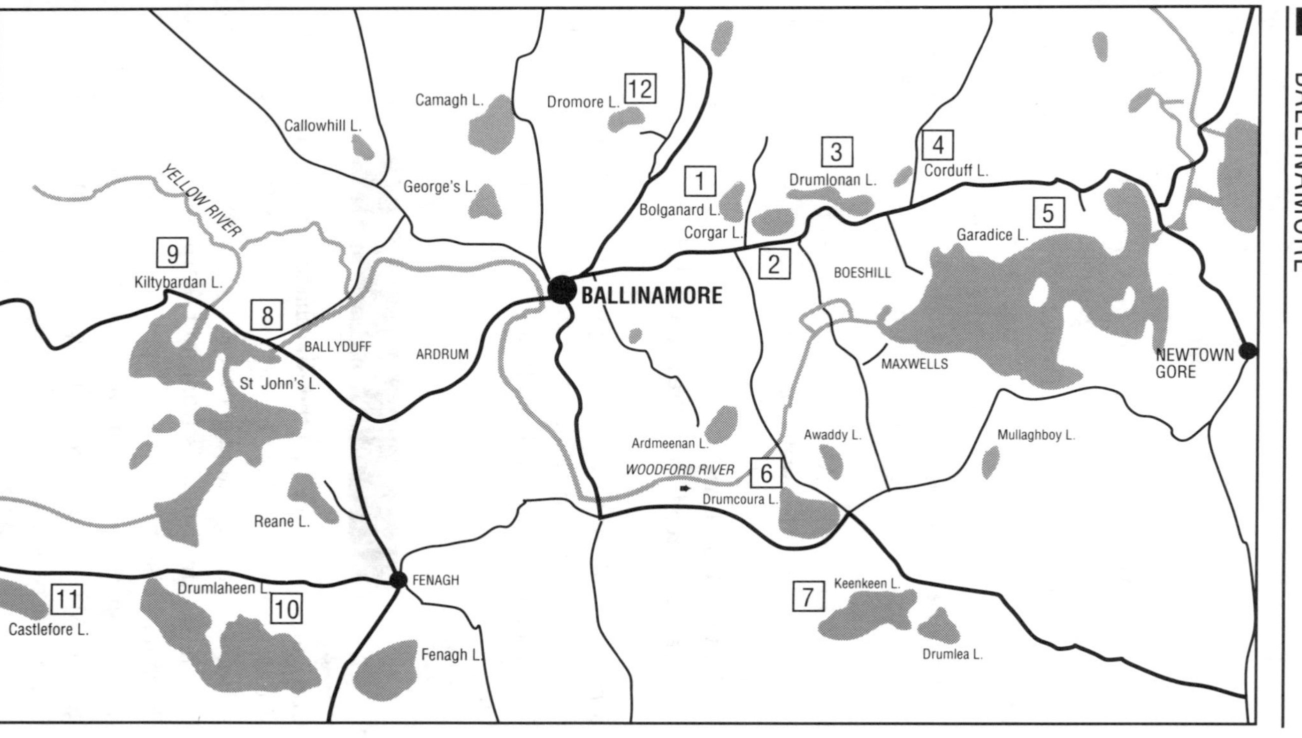
Camagh L.
Dromore L.
12
Callowhill L.
George's L.
1
Bolganard L.
Corgar L.
3
Drumlonan L.
4
Corduff L.
5
Garadice L.
YELLOW RIVER
9
Kiltybardan L.
8
BALLYDUFF
ARDRUM
BALLINAMORE
2
BOESHILL
MAXWELLS
NEWTOWN GORE
St John's L.
Ardmeenan L.
Awaddy L.
Mullaghboy L.
WOODFORD RIVER
6
Drumcoura L.
Reane L.
FENAGH
7
Keenkeen L.
Drumlaheen L.
10
11
Castlefore L.
Fenagh L.
Drumlea L.

8. ST JOHN'S LAKE: This water has access at several places with good parking. The lake has two sections, with a big stock of small Bream and Roach. This water beside the Carrick road has an abundance of Perch, with Pike and Eels.
9. KILTYBARDAN LAKE: Beside the Carrick road, with easy access and parking. There is a good stock of Bream here to 2.5 lbs (1 kg), with Roach, Hybrids, Perch, Pike and Eels.
10. DRUMLAHEEN LAKE: A big lake approached from Fenagh, the access and parking are easy. The bank is suitable for disabled anglers. There is a fair stock of Bream to 5 lbs (2.2 kg) here, with Roach, Hybrids, Perch, Pike and Eels.
11. CASTLEFORE LAKE: Beside the Fenagh-Keshcarrigan road, this reeded water has some swims for Bream, Roach, Perch, Pike and Eels.
12. DROMORE LAKE: This lake off the Ballinamore-Swanlinbar road holds Bream, Roach, Hybrids, Perch, Pike and Eels.

Special note: Major work is in progress on the Woodford River in restoring the canal. From Ballinamore via Ballyconnell, fishing on this water will be affected in many places for some time.

CARRIGALLEN

Carrigallen is situated on the Killeshandra-Mohill road (R201) about 12 miles (19 km) to the west of Cavan. The town is surrounded by lakes and is near Arva and Killeshandra in Co. Cavan. Bream fishing is from mid April to October. Roach, Perch and Pike provide good sport throughout the year, but the big fish come mostly in the colder months. Tench fishing is good in May/June and also in September. Fishing in this area is in a variety of lakes.

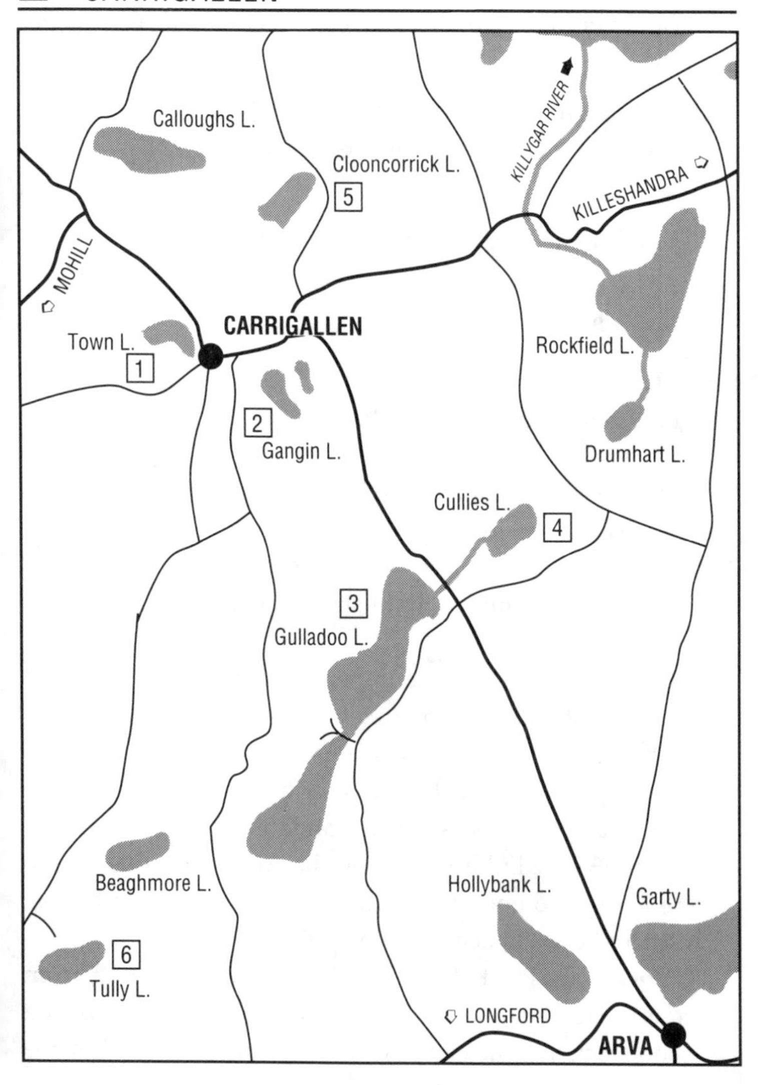

CLUBS

Carrigallen Tourist Development Association, Mrs Greta O'Neill, Main Street, Carrigallen, Tel (049) 39738.

ANGLING CONTACTS

Hotel and guesthouse owners are experienced in dealing with anglers.

TACKLE SHOP

Jack O'Neill, Main Street, Carrigallen, Tel (049) 39738.

BAIT

Jack O'Neill, Main Street, Carrigallen, Tel (049) 39738.

OTHER WATERS IN THIS AREA

See Arva, Killeshandra, Ballinamore, Gowna.

SPECIES

Bream, Roach, Hybrids, Tench, Perch, Pike, Eels.

1. TOWN LAKE: Fishing here is from stands. The lake holds some Tench to 5 lbs (2.2 kg) with some Roach and Perch.
2. GANGIN LAKE: Access is easy to this lake in the town. The swims are limited, but fishing is fair for Roach, Bream and Perch.
3. GULLADOO LAKE: The upper lake, over the bridge and to the right, has a short stretch for Bream and Roach. The best Bream in the lower lake are at the narrow part, where great catches of Roach and Hybrids are taken. This lake also holds good stocks of Perch and Pike.
4. CULLIES LAKE: Further along the Arva road, this lake to the left is also good for Bream to 4 lbs (1.8 kg), with a big stock of Perch, Roach, Pike and Eels.
5. CLOONCORRICK LAKE: This lake, with fishing from stands, holds some good Tench to 6 lbs (2.7 kg), with a good stock of Roach and Perch. The water also holds some Bream, Pike and Eels. This lake is approached off the Killeshandra road to the left.
6. TULLY LAKE: Off the Moyne road at 3 miles (4.8 km), this is a good water producing good Bream catches, with fish to 4 lbs (1.8 kg). It also holds Roach, Hybrids, Perch, Pike and Eels.

CARRICK-ON-SHANNON

Carrick-on-Shannon is the principal town in Co. Leitrim and is situated on the Dublin-Sligo road (N4). The River Shannon flows through the town, which has all facilities, including a marina for cruisers. Fishing in this area is in lakes and rivers.

Bream and Roach fishing is good from late April to October, but Roach are best in the spring and autumn months. Pike fishing is good throughout the year, with the colder months producing the best results.

CLUBS

Carrick-on-Shannon Angling and Tourism Development Association, Secretary, Mrs J. Conefry, Canal View, Keshcarrigan, Tel (078) 42056.

ANGLING CONTACTS

Guesthouse and hotel owners in this area are experienced in dealing with anglers.

TACKLE SHOPS

The Creel, Main Street, Carrick, Tel (078) 20166.
Holts Tackle Shop, Bridge Street, Carrick, Tel (078) 20184.
Geraghty's, Main Street, Carrick.
Aisleigh House, Dublin Road, Carrick, Tel (078) 20313.

BAIT

Sean Ferron, Aisleigh House, Carrick, Tel (078) 20313.
The Creel, Main Street, Carrick, Tel (078) 20166.

OTHER WATERS IN THIS AREA

See Boyle, Drumshanbo, Mohill, Ballinamore, Roosky.

SPECIES

Bream, Roach, Rudd, Hybrid, Perch, Pike, Eels, Tench.

BOATS

M. Lynch, Villa Moria, Carrick, Tel (078) 20034.

S. Ferron, Aisleigh House, Carrick, Tel (078) 20313.

CARRICK-ON-SHANNON

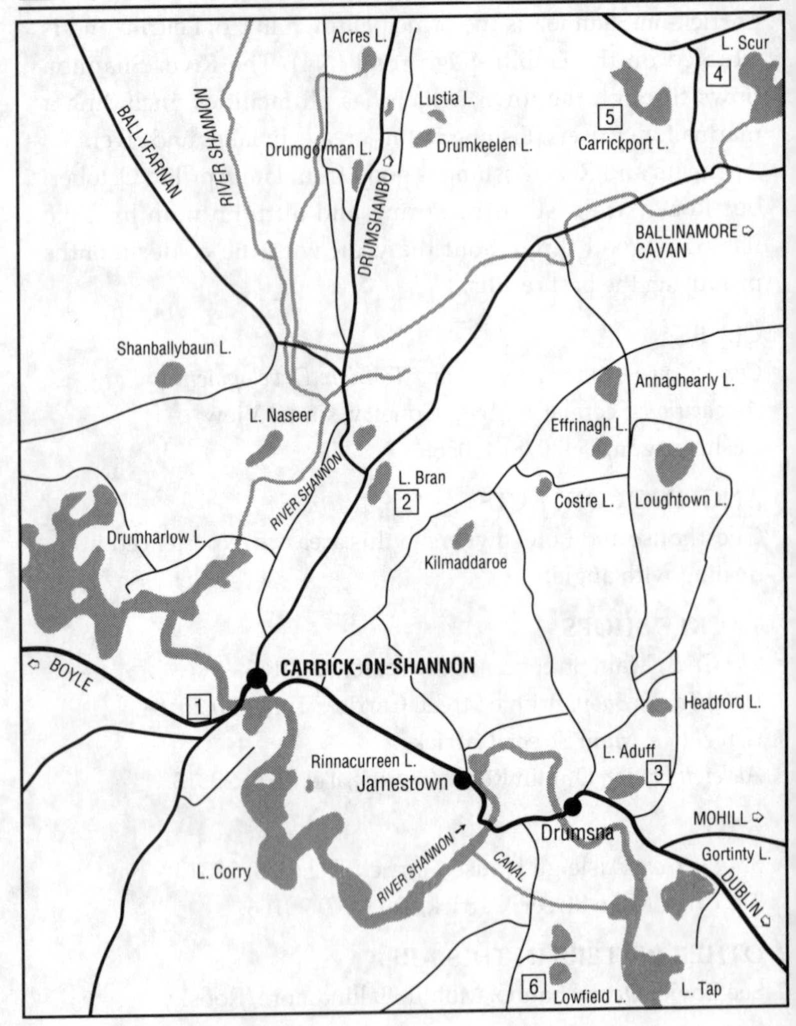

1. RIVER SHANNON: The river above Carrick has good Bream fishing, particularly at Hartley Bridge. In Carrick, there is good Bream and Roach fishing from the stands provided along the western bank and down to the bridge. There are many good angling spots below the town for quality Bream, Roach, Rudd and Hybrids, especially at Jamestown and Drumsna. The river, all along this area, is good for Pike and Perch fishing, with Roach and Eels.
2. LOUGH BRAN: This is a small but good fishery beside the Ballinamore road, with Bream to 4 lbs (1.8 kg), Roach, Hybrids, Perch and Tench to 5 lbs (2.2 kg).
3. LOUGH ADUFF: South of Drumsna, beside the Longford road, this good Tench water has fish to 5 lbs (2.2 kg). It also has a big stock of Roach, Rudd and Perch.
4. LOUGH SCUR: The access off the Ballinamore road leads to a good fishing stretch where there is an abundance of Bream to 2.5 lbs (1 kg) with Roach, Perch and Pike. This lake is also fishable from a stretch accessible from the Keshcarrigan road.
5. CARRICKPORT LAKE: Access is easy on the roadside bank. Fishing is for Bream, Roach, Perch and Pike.
   KESHCARRIGAN LAKE: This lake, 12 miles (19 km) from Carrick, has a good access and fishing is from stands. The lake holds a good stock of Bream to 4 lbs (1.8 kg) and some Roach. There are also Perch, Pike and Eels here. This lake is off the map to the right and is near Keshcarrigan village.
6. LOWFIELDLOUGH: There is good fishing for Tench to 6 lbs (2.7 kg) in May and June.

DRUMSHANBO

Drumshanbo is south of Lough Allen and upriver on the River Shannon from Carrick on the R280 road. This is a small town in a scenic area between two mountains and dominated by the first big lake on the Shannon, Lough Allen. Fishing in this area is in lakes and the River Shannon.

Pike fishing is good here all year, but the best results come in the colder months. Bream fishing commences in mid April and continues to October. Roach feed throughout the year. Tench are at their best in May-June.

CLUBS

Lough Allen Angling Club, Ari Elbersee, Carrick Road, Tel (078) 41139.

Lough Allen Conservation Association, Sean Wynne, Drumkerrin Road, Drumshanbo.

ANGLING CONTACTS

Ari Elbersee, Knitella Ltd, Carrick Road, Tel (078) 41139.

All hotel and guesthouse owners are experienced in dealing with anglers.

TACKLE SHOPS

See Carrick-on-Shannon.

BAIT

See Carrick-on-Shannon.

Lough Scur Bait and Tackle, Kilclare, Tel (078) 41438.

OTHER WATERS IN THIS AREA

See Boyle, Carrick-on-Shannon and Ballinamore.

SPECIES

Bream, Roach, Pike, Perch, Eels, Tench.

BOATS

O'Dwyer's, Lakeside House, Cornashamoge, Tel (078) 41112.

Lough Allen Community Boats, Brian McGourty, Carrick Road, Drumshanbo.

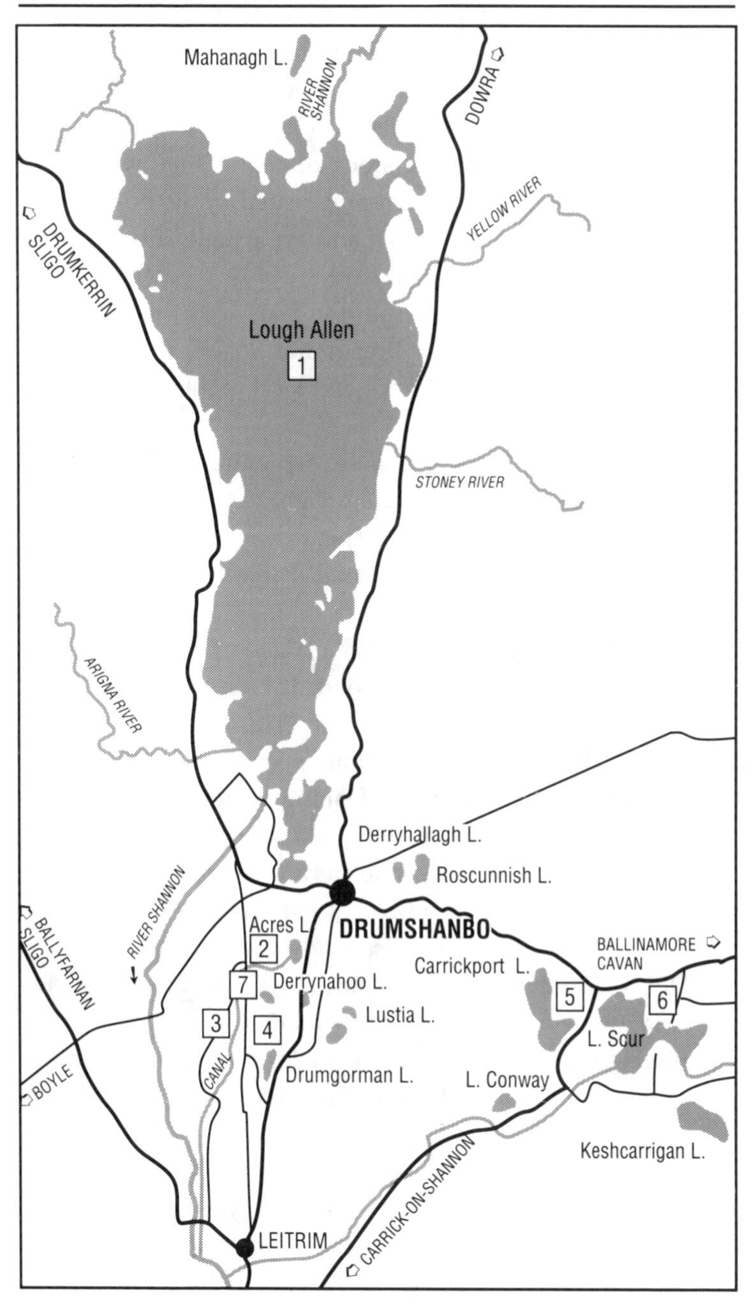
Mahanagh L.
RIVER SHANNON
DOWRA
DRUMKERRIN SLIGO
YELLOW RIVER
Lough Allen
1
STONEY RIVER
ARIGNA RIVER
Derryhallagh L.
Roscunnish L.
RIVER SHANNON
BALLYFARNAN SLIGO
Acres L.
DRUMSHANBO
2
BALLINAMORE CAVAN
Carrickport L.
7
Derrynahoo L.
5
6
3
Lustia L.
4
L. Scur
CANAL
BOYLE
Drumgorman L.
L. Conway
CARRICK-ON-SHANNON
Keshcarrigan L.
LEITRIM

1. LOUGH ALLEN: This is a big, deep lake and one of Ireland's leading big Pike waters, holding good specimen fish. It is best fished throughout the year by trolling. But in the early months, Pike are located in the bays when they can be fished from the bank.

   The lake holds a big stock of coarse fish, with some good Brown Trout. Bream are located in the bottom and shallow section of the lake and are usually fished at the point near the Drumkerrin road.

   The River Shannon, from the lake to 300 m below the sluice gates, is good for Bream and Roach. This stretch is controlled as a Trout fishery and local regulations must be adhered to.
2. ACRES LAKE: This small water along the Carrick road has some Roach, Perch and small Bream.
3. LOUGH ALLEN CANAL: This is a narrow and shallow water which holds Roach, small Perch, small Bream and some Tench.
4. DRUMGORMAN LAKE: This is a good fishery, with easy access beside the Carrick road. It holds good stocks of Bream and Roach, with Perch and Pike.
5. CARRICKPORT LAKE: Parking is along the narrow, busy Carrick-Ballinamore road. Fishing is from the bank and stands for Bream, Roach, Perch, Pike and Eels.
6. LOUGH SCUR: This big lake has access off the Ballinamore road. Fishing from the rocky bank is good for Bream, Roach, Perch, Pike, Hybrids.
7. DERRYNAHOO LAKE: Beside the Drumshanbo-Carrick road; good for Bream, Hybrids and Roach.

   BELHAVEL LAKE: This lovely lake near Drumkerrin has some Bream, Pike and Perch. Easy access and parking.

MOHILL

Mohill is located to the east of the Shannon system, south of Ballinamore. It is near some of the lakes attached to the River Erne. Fishing is in many lakes and a river.

Mohill is a small market town with many lakes nearby. Bream fishing comes on from mid April to October, and Tench fishing is best in May and June. Rudd feed freely on the hot summer days. Roach feed throughout the whole year but are best in the colder months. Pike fishing is over the year but is best in the winter.

CLUBS

Mohill Angling Club, Mrs Veronica Mitchell, Drumbo, Mohill.

ANGLING CONTACTS

Mrs M. Maloney, Glebe House, and also Lough Rinn House and Gardens, Mohill, Tel (078) 31086.

Hotel and guesthouse owners are experienced in dealing with anglers.

TACKLE SHOPS

See Carrick-on-Shannon and Ballinamore.

BAIT

John Maloney, Glebe House, Mohill, Tel (078) 31086.

OTHER WATERS IN THIS AREA

See Carrick-on-Shannon, Ballinamore, Strokestown, Roosky.

SPECIES

Bream, Roach, Rudd, Hybrids, Tench, Perch, Pike, Eels.

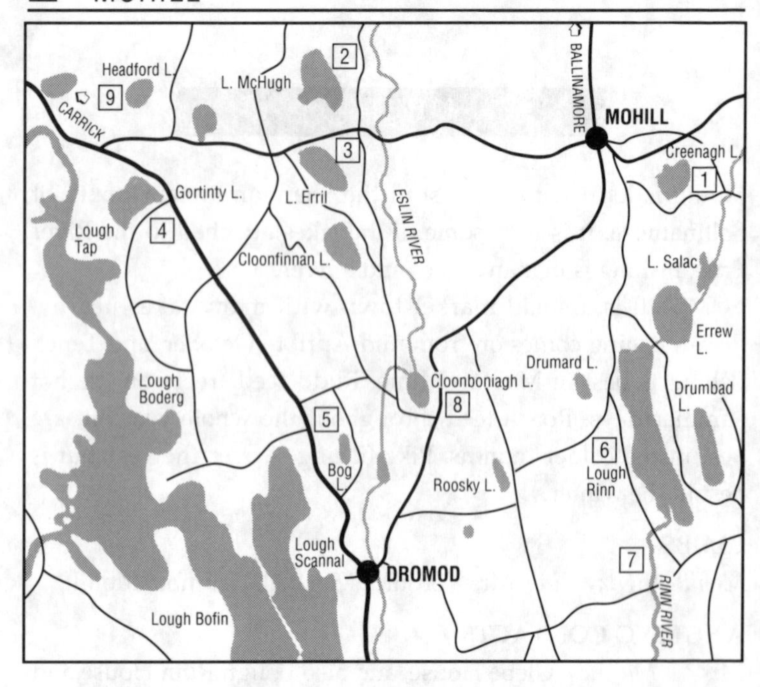

1. CREENAGH LAKE: This lake just 1 mile (1.6 km) south of the town has easy access and fishing is from stands. It holds Tench to 6 lbs (2.7 kg) with Bream to 3 lbs (1.3 kg) and Roach. It also has an abundance of Perch, with Pike and Eels.
2. LOUGH McHUGH: This is a rich water with lakeside parking. It has stocks of good Bream and Rudd. It also holds Hybrids, Perch, Pike and Eels. This water is approached off the Carrick road at 3 miles (4.8 km) and near Eslin Bridge.
3. LOUGH ERRIL: This is a heavily-weeded water beside the Mohill-Carrick road which holds Tench. A shallow water, it is difficult to fish, but the reward could be specimen Tench to 7 lbs (3 kg).
4. GORTINTY LAKE: This big lake is near the Shannon beside the Longford road. It has some swims for good Bream, Rudd, Perch, Roach, Pike and Eels.

5. BOG LAKE: This lake is off the Carrick-Longford road near Dromod. It produces good catches of Tench, with some Roach, Perch and Pike.
6. LOUGH RINN: 3 miles (4.8 km) from Mohill, this is a big lake with shallow margins on the west side. Fishing is from stands for Tench, Roach, Bream, Rudd, Perch, Pike and Eels. There is access from Lough Rinn House and Gardens, where there is a small charge for admission.
7. RINN RIVER: This is a sluggish river with good Roach fishing in the winter and spring. It also has small Bream, Perch and Pike.
8. CLOONBONIAGH LAKE: 3 miles (4.8 km) from Mohill, this lake has easy access to fishing from stands. Shallow and weedy, it holds small Bream, Roach, Perch and Pike.
9. HEADFORD LAKE: Located near the road, this lake has fishing from stands for Bream to 4 lbs (1.8 kg). It also has Perch, Roach, Pike and Eels.

County Limerick

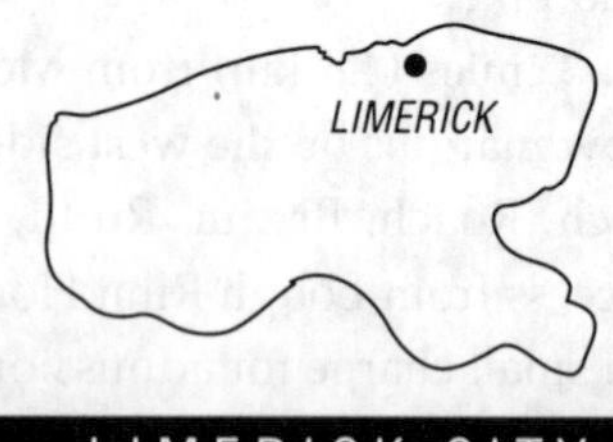

LIMERICK CITY

Limerick city is located at the bottom of the River Shannon, 120 miles (143 km) from Dublin.

Limerick is a city with all modern facilities for golf, tennis, swimming and other sports. The river flows through the city to enter the Shannon estuary, which is about 40 miles (64 km) long. Bream fishing is good from mid April to October. Rudd feed in the summer months, giving good sport. Perch and Pike are also present, with Pike fishing at its best in the colder months. Roach feed all year but provide best sport in the winter and spring. Fishing here is mostly in the River Shannon.

CLUB

Limerick Coarse Angling Club.

TACKLE SHOP

Joe Maloney, Riverside House, O'Brien's Bridge, Limerick, Tel (061) 377303.

Jim Robinson, Tackle Shop, Thomond Shopping Centre, Limerick, Tel (061) 44900.

BAIT

Joe Maloney, Riverside House, O'Brien's Bridge, Limerick, Tel (061) 377303.

OTHER WATERS IN THIS AREA

See O'Brien's Bridge, Tulla.

SPECIES

Bream, Rudd, Roach, Hybrids, Perch, Pike, Eels.

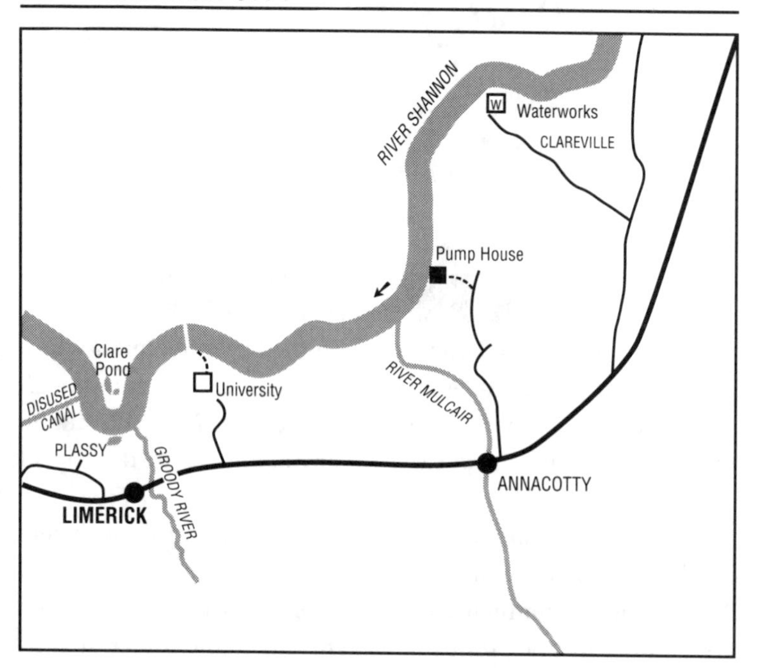

RIVER SHANNON: The river at Plassy produces hugh catches of Bream to 5 lbs (2.2 kg), the best locations being near the navigation posts. There are also Rudd, Perch and some Pike here. Upriver at the pump house near Annacotty, there is another great stretch of river for Bream, Rudd, Roach, Hybrids, Perch, Pike and Eels. Above this point, approachable from near Castleconnell, there are good Roach in the colder months below the Clareville stretch.

Upriver from here lies the O'Brien's Bridge stretch (see O'Brien's Bridge).

Special Note: The River Shannon in this area is a mixed fishery, with Salmon and Trout present in private stretches. The waters are controlled by the ESB and anglers should exercise care in fishing only designated coarse fishing stretches. Advice on waters can be obtained locally.

County Longford

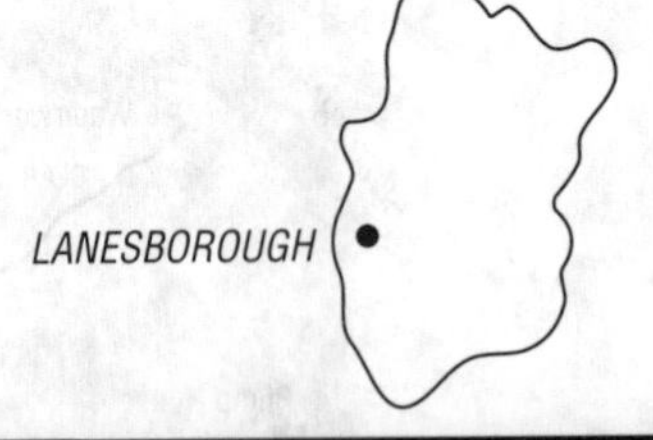

LANESBOROUGH

Lanesborough in Co. Longford is on the River Shannon which divides it from the village of Ballyleague in Co. Roscommon. It is located on the Longford-Roscommon road (N63). Fishing in this area is primarily on the River Shannon and the top of Lough Ree.

The village is situated above Lough Ree and the river here can be very busy with cruising traffic in summer. Bream and Tench fishing commences in late April, but the town stretch goes off in July and August. Roach fishing in the colder months is good. Pike fishing in the lake is good all year, but the best months are from September to March. There is an abundance of Perch here.

CLUB

Lanesborough CAC, Michael Wyse, Tel (043) 21503.

ANGLING CONTACTS

Michael Wyse, Pricewyse, Lanesborough, Tel (043) 21503.

Hotel and guesthouse owners are experienced in dealing with anglers.

TACKLE SHOP

Michael Wyse, Pricewyse, Lanesborough.

Mrs Holmes, Lakeside Store, Main Street, Tel (043) 21491.

BAIT

Mrs Holmes, Lakeside Store.

Michael Wyse, Pricewyse, Lanesborough, Tel (043) 21503.

OTHER WATERS IN THIS AREA

See also Tarmonbarry, Castlecoote, Athlone.

SPECIES

Bream, Rudd, Roach, Hybrids, Tench, Perch, Pike, Eels.

BOATS

Eamon Ryan, Bungalow, Lanesborough.

LANESBOROUGH

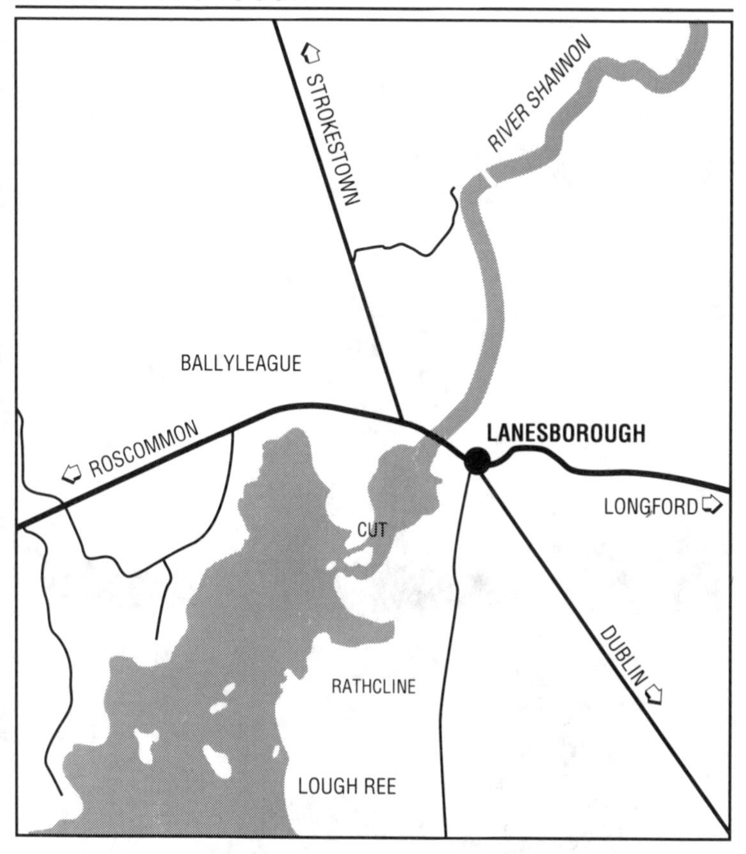

RIVER SHANNON: The river is wide here, with a good fishing stretch along the left bank. The hot water effluent from the power station above the bridge influences the fishing. It holds specimen Bream, Tench to 7 lbs (3 kg), Rudd, Roach, Hybrids in April, May and June. Small Perch are common here. Roach fishing is good in the colder months.

LOUGH REE: This big lake is best fished from a boat. It has an abundance of large specimen-sized coarse fish, including Bream, Rudd, Roach, Hybrids, Tench, Perch, Pike and Eels. The 'Cut', just out from Lanesborough, can be fished easily, as it is not exposed to the strong winds one can expect on this big water.

County Meath

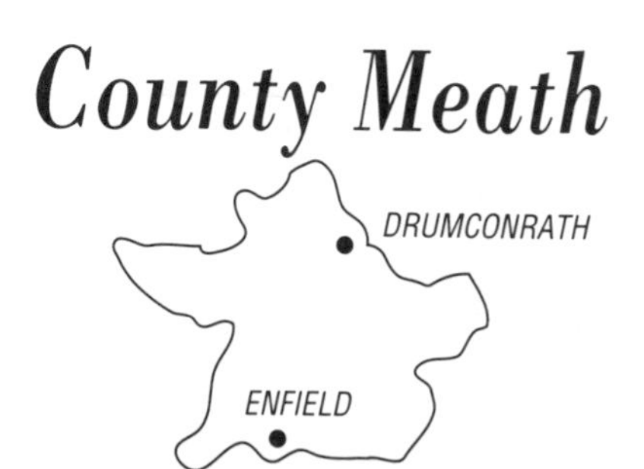

DRUMCONRATH

Drumconrath is situated about 5 miles (8 km) west of Ardee which is on the N2 from Dublin to Monaghan. It is a small town in the north-eastern corner of Co. Meath, 40 miles (64 km) from Dublin. Bream fishing is good from mid April to October. Rudd feed in the summer months. Roach, Perch and Pike provide fishing throughout the year. Tench fishing is best in the early summer months. Fishing in this area is in lakes only.

CLUB

Drumconrath Angling Development Association, Larry Ward, Inis Fail, Drumconrath, Tel (041) 54161.

ANGLING CONTACTS

Guesthouse owners in this area are experienced in dealing with anglers.

TACKLE SHOP

Jimmy McMahon, Carrick Sports Shop, Carrickmacross, Tel (042) 61714.

BAIT

J. McMahon, Carrick Sports Shop, Carrickmacross.

OTHER WATERS IN THIS AREA

See Carrickmacross, Kingscourt, Castleblayney, Bailieborough.

SPECIES

Bream, Roach, Rudd, Hybrids, Tench, Perch, Pike, Eels.

COMPETITION

Drumconrath Festival – July.

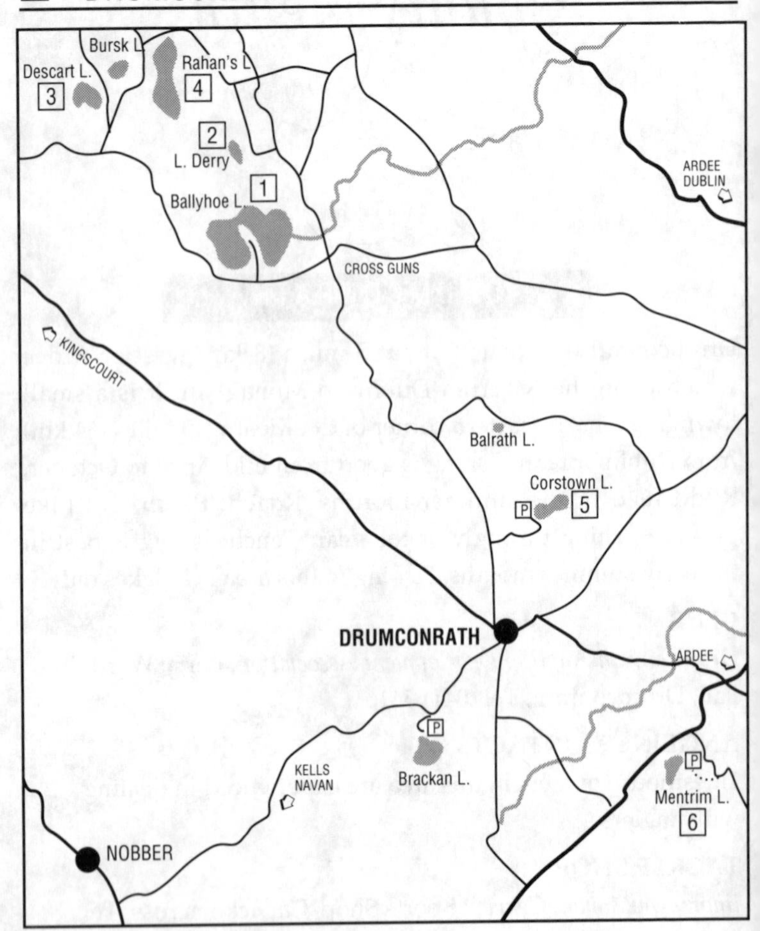

1. BALLYHOE LAKE: This lake, off the Carrickmacross road at the Cross Guns, has good access near the football pitch. The first of two lakes, it has good banks and produces good catches of Tench to 6 lbs (2.7 kg) in May/June, with Bream, Rudd, Perch, Pike and Eels. Ballyhoe Lake 2 is weedy in the summer and holds Roach and Rudd, with good Hybrids. This water also holds Tench to 6 lbs (2.7 kg). Access to this lake is from the opposite side to the football pitch.

2. LOUGH DERRY: Near Ballyhoe Lake 2, this rich lake with firm banks has a good stock of Bream to 9 lbs (4 kg), with some Tench, Roach, Rudd, Hybrids, Perch and Pike.
3. DESCART LAKE: There is a waterside car park and fishing is to the left of this lake which lies between Drumconrath and Carrickmacross near Kingscourt. There is a big stock of Roach, Rudd and Hybrids here. The lake also has Perch and good Bream fishing.
4. RAHAN'S LAKE: This lake is near Descart Lake and holds good stocks of Bream, with Roach, Perch and Pike.
5. CORSTOWN LAKE: This 30-acre lake is 1 mile (1.6 km) from the village. There is waterside parking, and fishing is accessible all round the lake. A muddy lake, fishing is from stands. It holds good stocks of Bream, Roach, some Rudd, Hybrids, Perch, Pike, Eels.
6. MENTRIM LAKE: East of Drumconrath, this water of 10 acres has waterside parking. Fishing here is for good Bream to 7 lbs (3 kg) and also Tench to 6 lbs (2.7 kg). It also holds Roach, Perch, Pike and Eels.

ENFIELD

Enfield is situated on the Dublin-Galway (N4) road, about 25 miles (40 km) outside Dublin. The village lies alongside the southern bank of the canal. Roach and Perch fishing provide sport throughout the year. Tench fishing with Rudd is best in the summer months.

CLUBS

Enfield Coarse Angling Club, Brian Donoghue, Enfield.

ANGLING CONTACT

Brian Donoghue, Enfield.

TACKLE SHOP

Countryside Angling, Pacelli Road, Naas.

Rory Harkin, 17a Temple Bar, Dublin 2.

BAIT

See Tackle shop.

OTHER WATERS IN THIS AREA

See Prosperous, Mullingar, Athy.

SPECIES

Roach, Tench, Rudd, Bream, Hybrids, Perch, Eels.

■ ENFIELD

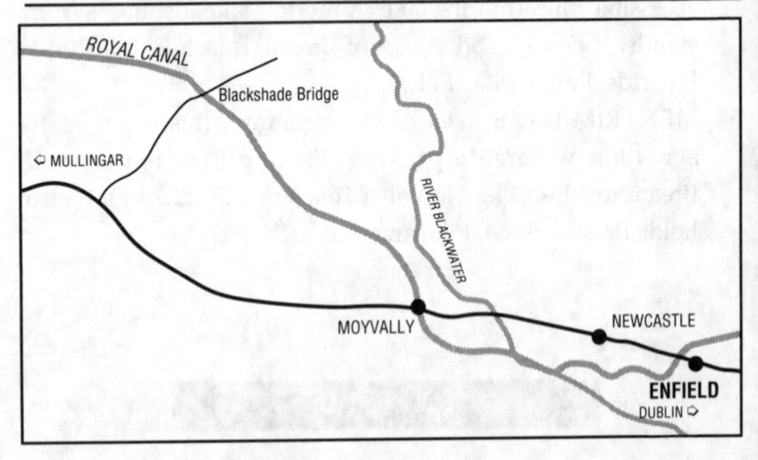

ROYAL CANAL: From Dublin, there are long stretches of the canal which are shallow, weedy and overgrown. Here local anglers find Tench in some swims.

In Maynooth harbour, there are some Carp to 6 lbs (2.7 kg). There is also some good fishing around the new harbour in Kilcock. From Cloncurry bridge to Ferns Lock 17, the stretch provides good fishing for Roach, Rudd, Hybrids, Tench, Perch, Pike and Eels. From Blackshade bridge to Hill of Down, the canal gives good sport for Bream and Tench over most of the year. There are also Rudd, Hybrids, Perch, some Pike and Eels.

County Monaghan

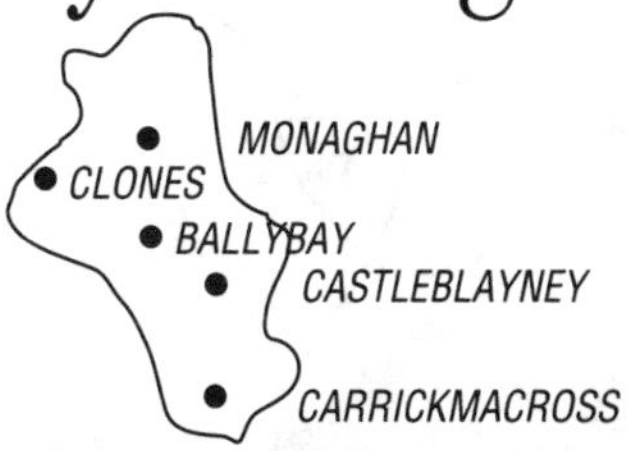

MONAGHAN
CLONES
BALLYBAY
CASTLEBLAYNEY
CARRICKMACROSS

BALLYBAY

Ballybay is situated on the Cootehill-Castleblayney road on the shores of Lough Major. The River Dromore flows through the town and forms numerous lakes in which there is an abundance of coarse fish. Bream fishing comes into its own from mid April to October. Roach, Perch and Pike provide sport throughout the year, with the best fish coming in the colder months. Fishing here is in many lakes and the Dromore River.

CLUB

Ballybay Tourist Development Association, Talbot Duffy, Main Street, Ballybay, Tel (042) 41692.

ANGLING CONTACTS

Guesthouse owners are experienced in dealing with anglers.

TACKLE SHOPS

Martin O'Kane, Main Street, Ballybay, Tel (042) 41022.

BAIT

C.J. Fay, Cabragh House, Cootehill, Tel (049) 52153.

OTHER WATERS IN THIS AREA

See Cootehill and Castleblayney.

SPECIES

Bream, Roach, Hybrids, Perch, Pike, Eels, Tench, Rudd.

COMPETITIONS

Ballybay Festival – May.
Co. Monaghan Pairs Festival – September.

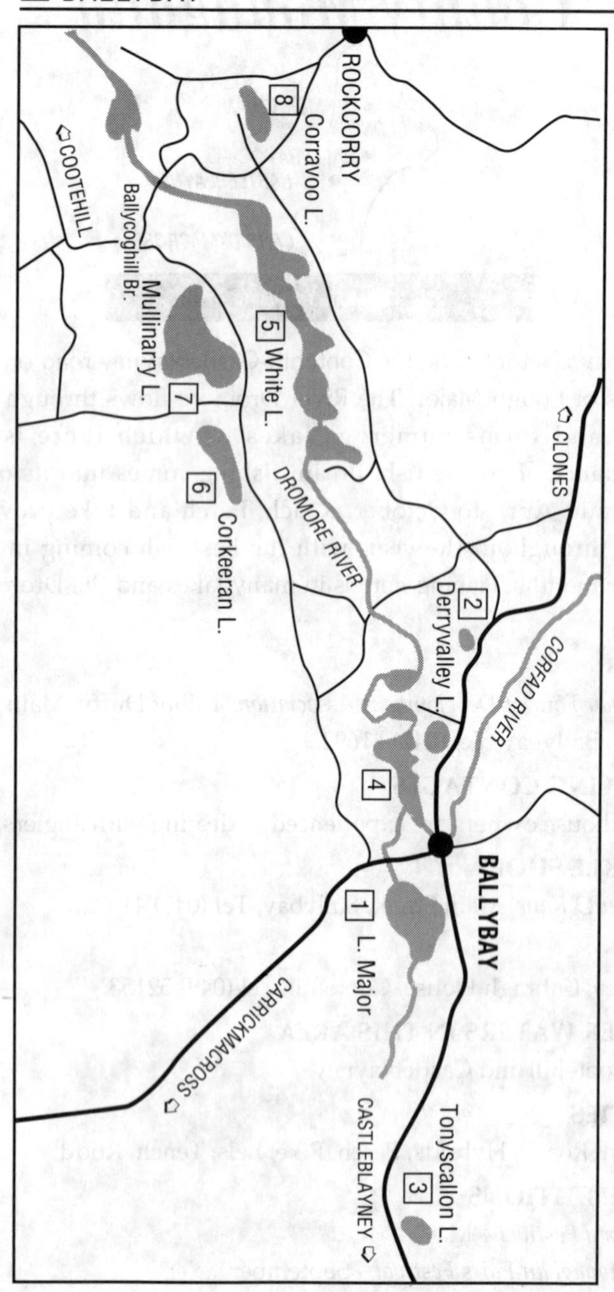
ROCKCORRY
8
Corravoo L.
COOTEHILL
Ballycoghill Br.
Mullinarry L.
5
White L.
7
6
Corkeeran L.
DROMORE RIVER
CLONES
2
Derryvalley L.
CORFAD RIVER
4
BALLYBAY
1
L. Major
CARRICKMACROSS
CASTLEBLAYNEY
Tonyscallon L.
3

1. LOUGH MAJOR: This is a big lake with easy access near the town. There is a big stock of Bream to 3 lbs (1.3 kg) in it, with Roach, Hybrids and Perch also. This good fishery also holds Pike.
2. DERRYVALLEY LAKE: A small lake along the Clones road, with some Roach and Perch. It also has some small Tench which are caught in May/June.
3. TONYSCALLON LAKE: This lake is beside the Castleblayney road. Access is easy from the parking area. The water holds Bream, Roach, Hybrids, Perch, Pike and Eels.
4. DROMORE RIVER AND LAKES: Flowing from Lough Major, this river forms several lakes scattered over low-lying ground off the Clones road. The margins are reeded and fishing is from stands and from some clear banks. There is a big stock of Bream in this area, with Roach, Hybrids, Perch and Pike. Some Tench also appear in Rectory Lake in May/June.
5. WHITE LAKE: There are two access points to this lake. One is at Baird's Shore where there is an abundance of small Bream, with Roach, Hybrids, Perch and Pike. There is further access down a field to the Bream Rock, where good results are also yielded. There are also Tench here.
6. CORKEERAN LAKE: Beside the Cootehill road, this lake has some swims for small Roach and Bream to 2.5 lbs (1 kg). It also has Hybrids, some Rudd, Perch, Pike and Eels.
7. MULLINARRY LAKE: This lake beside the Cootehill road is a fair fishery. It has a few Bream swims only, with some Roach, Pike, Perch and Eels.
8. CORRAVOO LAKE: Near Rockcorry, this is a good lake for Bream, Roach, Perch and Pike.

CARRICKMACROSS

Carrickmacross is on the N2, 45 miles (72 km) north of Dublin. This is a prosperous market town, with all facilities for tennis, golf, swimming etc. Bream in some waters come on in March and continue to feed into November. Rudd feed in the summer months. Tench fishing is good in the summer but is at its best in May/June. Roach, Perch and Pike provide good sport most times of the year, but during the colder months, the best Pike and Roach are taken. Fishing in this area is in lakes only.

CLUB

Carrickmacross Tourist Association, Mrs Nuala Russell, Nurebeg House, Carrickmacross, Tel (042) 61044.

ANGLING CONTACTS

Bill Reidy, Eastern Regional Fisheries Board, Creevy Lake, Tel (042) 61178.

Jimmy McMahon, Carrick Sports Shop, Carrickmacross.

Guesthouse owners are experienced in dealing with anglers.

TACKLE SHOP

Jimmy McMahon, Carrick Sports Shop, Carrickmacross, Tel (042) 61714.

BAIT

Jimmy McMahon, Carrick Sports Shop.

OTHER WATERS IN THIS AREA

See Castleblayney, Monaghan, Shercock.

SPECIES

Bream, Rudd, Roach, Hybrids, Tench, Perch, Pike, Eels.

COMPETITION

Farney Festival – May.

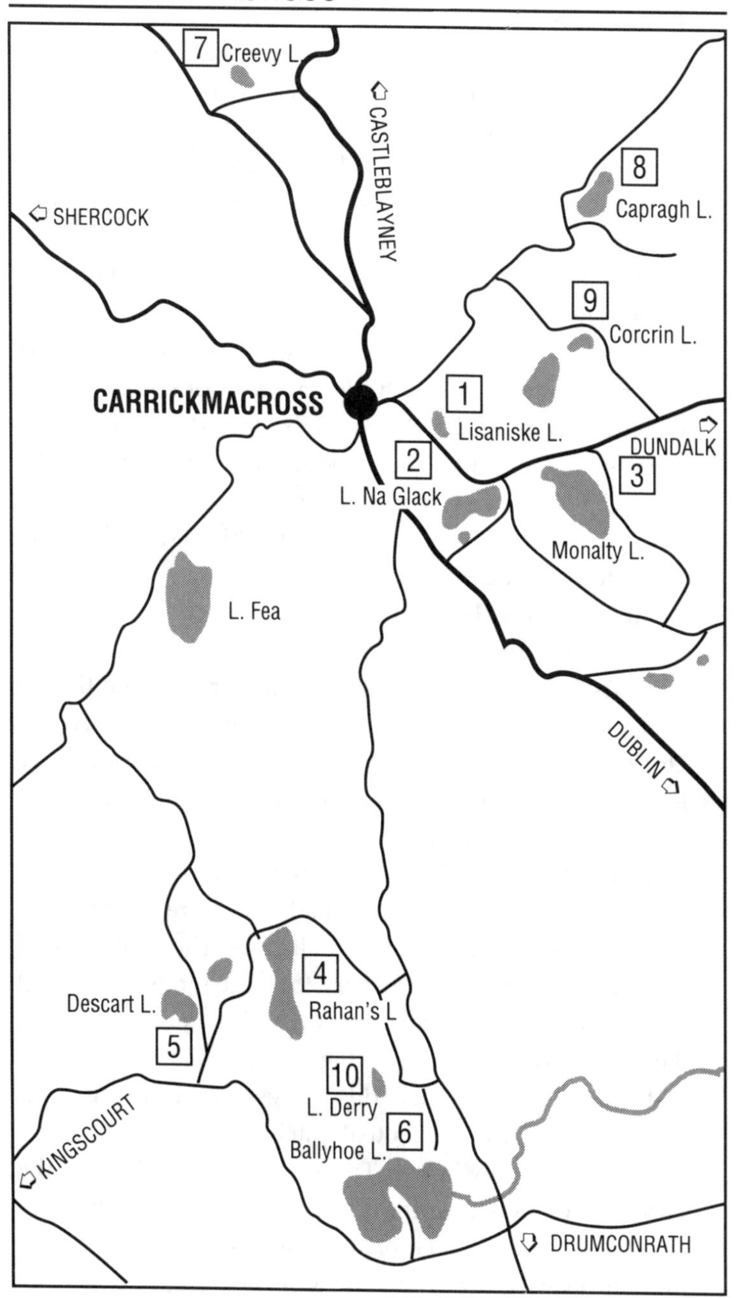
7
Creevy L.
CASTLEBLAYNEY
8
Capragh L.
SHERCOCK
9
Corcrin L.
CARRICKMACROSS
1
Lisaniske L.
DUNDALK
2
3
L. Na Glack
Monalty L.
L. Fea
DUBLIN
4
Descart L.
Rahan's L
5
10
L. Derry
KINGSCOURT
6
Ballyhoe L.
DRUMCONRATH

1. LISANISKE LAKE: This lake beside the town has fishing from stands for small Bream and Roach.
2. LOUGH NA GLACK: A rich water, 1 mile (1.6 km) from the town, which holds a good stock of specimen Bream to 10 lbs (4.5 kg), Rudd to 2 lbs (0.9 kg), Hybrids to 5 lbs (2.2 kg) and Tench to 6 lbs (2.7 kg). The banks are low and sometimes soft. Fishing is from stands in this wooded area. Fishing on this water has recently been affected by poor water quality, and enquiries should be made locally prior to fishing.
3. MONALTY LAKE: This is a shallow and often weedy water of 60 acres but with a great stock of specimen fish. Quality Bream, Rudd, Roach, Hybrids and Tench provide great sport here. Parking is beside the lake which is 1.5 miles (2.4 km) from Carrickmacross.
4. RAHAN'S LAKE: The surrounds to this 50-acre lake, off the Drumconrath road, are low and the banks in wet weather are soft. The lake has a good stock of Bream to 5 lbs (2.2 kg), with Roach, Perch and Pike.
5. DESCART LAKE: There is a waterside car park and fishing is to the left of this 17-acre lake which lies between Drumconrath and Carrickmacross near Kingscourt. There is a big stock of Roach, Rudd and Hybrids here. The lake also has Perch and good Bream fishing.
6. BALLYHOE LAKE: This lake near Drumconrath is off the Carrickmacross-Drumconrath road. There are actually two lakes and the first is at the football pitch. The bank is good and clear. This is a good fishery for Tench to 6 lbs (2.7 kg) in May/June, with Bream, Rudd, Pike, Perch and Eels. Ballyhoe Lake 2 is weedy in the summer and holds Roach and Rudd, with good Hybrids. Access to this lake is from the opposite side of the football pitch.
7. CREEVY LAKE: A Brown Trout fishery controlled by the Carrickmacross AC is off the Castleblayney road. This lake also holds a good stock of Rudd and Perch. Information from the Fisheries Office on the waterside.

8. CAPRAGH LAKE: This 26-acre water is 3 miles (4.8 km) from Carrick and has waterside parking. The depths vary and the shores are sometimes soft in places. Fishing is from stands. The rich lake holds good Bream to 9 lbs (4 kg) with Rudd, Roach, Tench, Hybrids, Perch, Pike and Eels.
9. CORCRIN LAKE: This 7-acre water beside the road is 3 miles (4.8 km) from Carrickmacross and is a good fishery. It holds good Tench, with Bream, Rudd, Roach, Hybrids, Pike and Eels.
10. LOUGH DERRY: A small but rich lake, with fishing on the west side only for quality Bream. It also holds Roach, Hybrids and Pike.

CASTLEBLAYNEY

Castleblayney is situated on the Dublin-Carrickmacross-Monaghan road (N2) about 12 miles (19 km) south of Monaghan. It is a busy town on the shores of the big Lough Muckno. Bream fishing is good from April to November. Roach, Perch and Pike provide sport throughout the year, with the big Pike results coming in the winter months. Fishing here is limited to lakes.

CLUB

Castleblayney Anglers Association, Frankie Poyntz, 17 Park Road, Drumillard, Castleblayney.

ANGLING CONTACTS

Guesthouse owners in this area are experienced in dealing with anglers.

TACKLE SHOPS

The Mascot, Castleblayney.
Jimmy McMahon, Carrick Sports Shop, Carrickmacross.

BAIT

Del Wilson, Hill View, Bree, Castleblayney, Tel (042) 46217.
Carrick Sports Shop, Carrickmacross, Tel (042) 61714.

OTHER WATERS IN THIS AREA

See Monaghan, Carrickmacross, Ballybay, Bailieborough.

SPECIES

Bream, Roach, Rudd, Hybrids, Tench, Perch, Pike, Eels.

CASTLEBLAYNEY

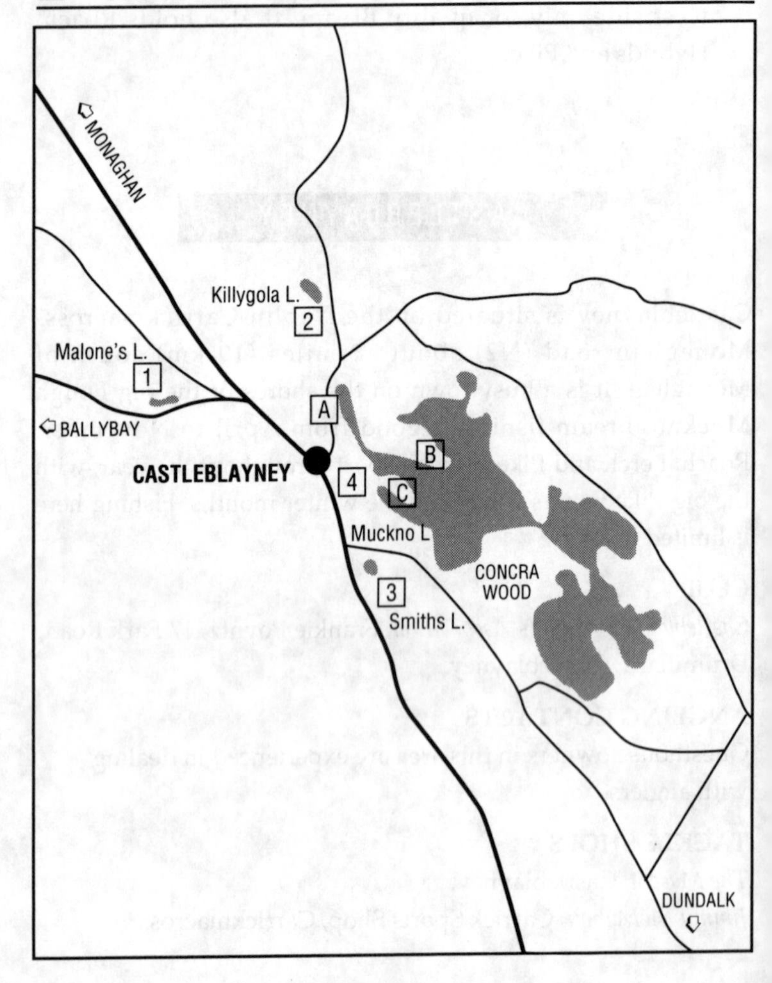

1. MALONE'S LAKE: Beside the Ballybay road, this reeded water of 10 acres has fishing from stands. It produces fair fishing for Bream, Roach, Perch, Pike, Eels.
2. KILLYGOLA LAKE: A 17-acre lake north of Castleblayney, where parking is dangerous along a winding road. There are Tench, Bream, Roach, Hybrids, Perch, Pike and Eels in this lake. Fishing is from stands, as some of the bank is soft.
3. SMITHS LAKE: This is a small water beside the Dundalk road. The margins are soft in this weedy water. It holds some Tench, Bream, Roach, Perch and Eels.
4. MUCKNO LAKE: This big lake of over 700 acres has fishing in many sections. It is under the control of Monaghan County Council and is used for other sports as well as angling.

A. GAS LAKE is situated on the inflowing stream behind Black Island, to the left, over the bridge and also off the Armagh Road in the town. Fishing here is good for Bream, Roach and Tench.

B. BLACK ISLAND: There is car parking at the bridge and foot access along the firm bank to the right. The fishing from the open bank provides good sport for Roach and Perch, with some good Pike in the winter months.

C. WHITE ISLAND lies to the right of the car park and is overlooked by the castle. The island has a good open bank. This section holds Roach, Bream, Perch, Pike and Eels.

CONCRA WOOD is situated midway along the western shore of the lake. Access to this forest is limited. At the end of the forest road, there are clear swims at the 'Belfast Steps', with fishing into 30 feet (9 m) for Bream, Roach and Pike. In other parts of the forest, there is fishing in shallower water (10 feet/3 m) for a variety of species. Toome stretch is in the eastern part of the lake. Here the bank is good and open, and fishing is for Bream, Roach, Hybrids, Perch, Pike and Eels. It is during the colder months that the big Pike give the best results here.

CLONES

Clones is situated north-east of Belturbet, close to the River Finn. It is a small, busy town surrounded by many lakes, all flowing into the Erne system. Bream fishing is from late April to October. Roach, Pike and Perch fishing is good throughout the year, but the best fish are taken in the winter months. Fishing in this area is in lakes and the River Finn.

CLUB

Clones and District Coarse Angling Club, Gerry McCaul, Newtownbutler Road, Clones.

ANGLING CONTACTS

Patrick Quigley, The Diamond Bar, Clones, Tel (047) 51229.

TACKLE SHOP

Terence Hanberry, Tackle Shop, Fermanagh Street, Clones. Tel (047) 51152.

BAIT

C.J. Fay, Cabragh House, Cootehill, Tel (049) 52153.

Irish Angling Services, Ardlougher, Ballyconnell, Tel (049) 26258.

OTHER WATERS IN THIS AREA

See Cootehill, Ballybay, Belturbet.

SPECIES

Bream, Roach, Hybrids, Rudd, Perch, Pike, Eels.

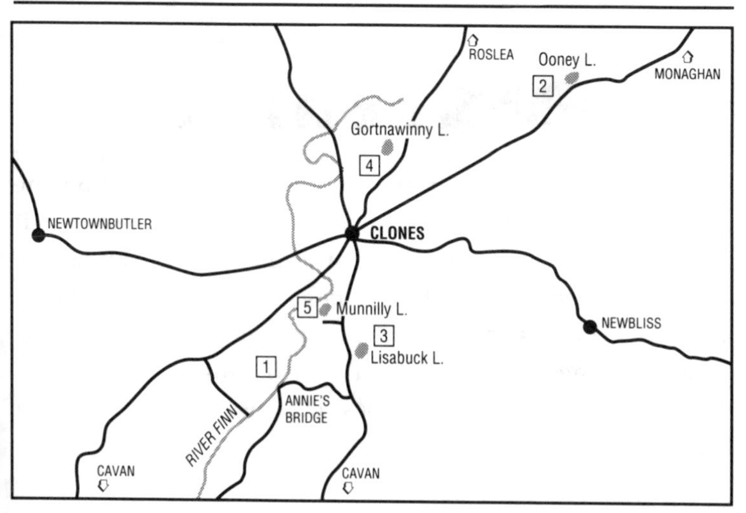

1. RIVER FINN: This is a slow moving and open river with a big stock of Roach, Perch, Rudd, Bream and Pike. Up and downstream at Annie's Bridge, off the Scotshouse road, there is good Roach fishing, with small Bream. There is an abundance of Perch here, with some Rudd and Pike. This river is used for matches, with a capacity for 100 anglers.
2. OONEY LAKE: Access is from the Clones-Monaghan road. Fishing is for good Roach, with Perch, Rudd, Hybrids, Pike.
3. LISABUCK LAKE: A good water just off the Scotshouse road, with a good stock of Roach, Perch, some Bream, Rudd, Hybrids and Pike. Access is easy to this reeded water.
4. GORTNAWINNY LAKE: Off the Roslea road with waterside parking, this weedy water holds a good stock of Roach, with Rudd, Hybrids, Perch and Pike.
5 MUNNILLY (CLONCALLIG) LAKE: This is a good water for Roach and Bream. Access is easy from roadside parking.

MONAGHAN

Monaghan, in the north of the county, is situated on the Dublin-Aughnacloy road (N2). The chief town of the county, it has all facilities, with tennis, golf, swimming etc. Bream fishing comes on in late April and continues to October. Roach, Perch and Pike fishing is good in the summer, with the best Pike and Roach coming in the winter. Tench fishing is good in the summer, with May/June the best months. Fishing here is in lakes only.

CLUB

Monaghan Anglers Club, S. McAleer, 4 Mall Road, Monaghan, Tel (047) 82454.

ANGLING CONTACTS

Seamus McAleer, 4 Mall Road, Monaghan.

Guesthouse and hotel owners are experienced in dealing with anglers.

TACKLE SHOP

Seamus McAleer, 4 Mall Road, Monaghan.

BAIT

Jimmy McMahon, Carrick Sports Shop, Carrick, Tel (042) 61714.

OTHER WATERS IN THIS AREA

See Castleblayney, Carrickmacross.

SPECIES

Bream, Roach, Rudd, Hybrids, Tench, Pike, Perch, Eels.

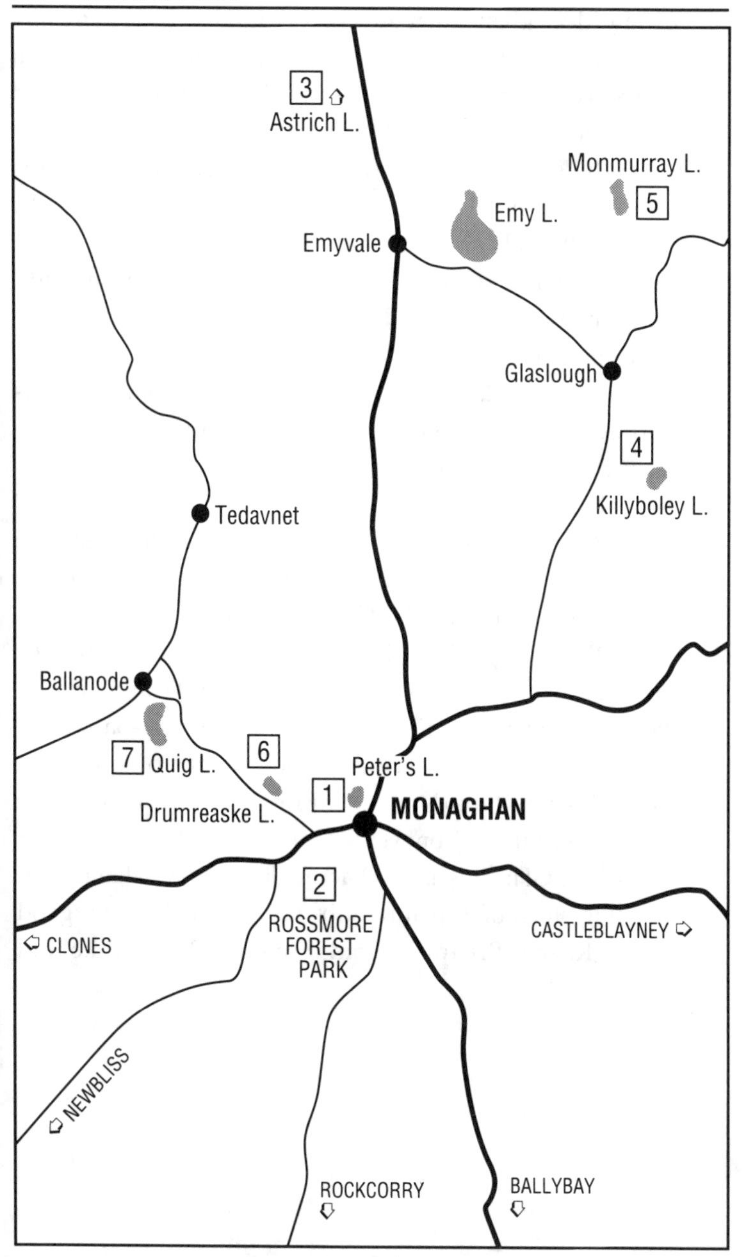
3
Astrich L.
Monmurray L.
Emy L.
5
Emyvale
Glaslough
4
Killyboley L.
Tedavnet
Ballanode
7
Quig L.
6
Drumreaske L.
Peter's L.
1
MONAGHAN
2
ROSSMORE
FOREST
PARK
CLONES
CASTLEBLAYNEY
NEWBLISS
ROCKCORRY
BALLYBAY

1. PETER'S LAKE: This small, shallow pond is situated within Monaghan town and is surrounded by an amenity area. The lakeside path and solid bank provide excellent access. Reeded in places, this water holds small Roach and Perch, with some Bream, Tench and Eels.
2. ROSSMORE FOREST PARK LAKES: Priestfield Lake is within the forest. This 7 acre lake is about 6–8 feet (1.8–2.4 m) deep. It holds an abundance of small Rudd.
   Castle Lake is a smaller lake. It has good fishing for Rudd and Tench and is located in the amenity area where the banks are good.
3. ASTRICH LAKE: North of Emyvale, this small water is cradled by hills. It has soft margins but in May/June produces good Tench fishing. It also has Rudd, Perch, Pike and Eels.
4. KILLYBOLEY LAKE: This 15-acre lake is near Glaslough and has some good fishing at times for Rudd and Tench to 4 lbs (1.8 kg). It also holds Pike, Perch and Eels.
5. MONMURRAY LAKE: Near Glaslough, this 25-acre lake offers fair fishing for Rudd, Bream, Perch, Pike and Eels.
6. DRUMREASKE LAKE: Beside the Monaghan-Ballanode road, this 10-acre fishery has good stocks of specimen Roach/Bream Hybrids, Roach, Bream, Tench, Perch, Pike and Eels. Fishing is from stands here.
7. QUIG LOUGH: This is a 30-acre lake beside Ballanode. It has a big stock of Tench to 6 lbs (2.7 kg) with some good Roach, Roach/Bream Hybrids, Bream, Perch, Pike and Eels.

County Offaly

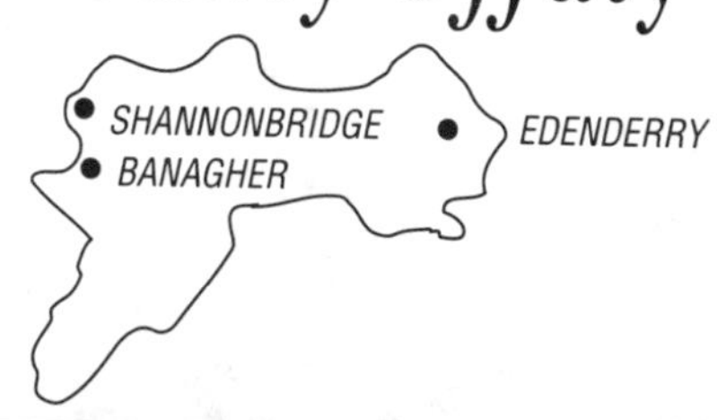

BANAGHER

Banagher is situated along the eastern bank of the River Shannon down from Shannon Harbour. This is a small town which has a busy marina in the summer months. A short distance above here, at Shannon Harbour, the Grand Canal and the River Brosna join the River Shannon from the east.

Bream and Rudd fishing are good over the summer months to October. Pike can be fished throughout the year, but the big fish are taken in the colder months. Tench fishing is best in May and June. Fishing here is in the River Shannon and Grand Canal.

CLUB

Banagher Angling Club, Joe Kennedy, Cula Cottage, Banagher.

ANGLING CONTACTS

Dermot Killeen, Shannonbridge, Tel (0905) 74112.

Guesthouse owners are experienced in dealing with anglers.

TACKLE SHOPS

Killeen's Shop, Shannonbridge.

Jim Griffin, Tackle Shop, Rahan, Tel (0506) 55979.

BAIT

Dermot Killeen, Shannonbridge.

Jim Griffin, Tackle Shop, Rahan.

OTHER WATERS IN THIS AREA

See Shannonbridge, Ballinasloe, Portumna.

SPECIES

Bream, Rudd, Hybrids, Perch, Pike, Tench, Eels.

BANAGHER

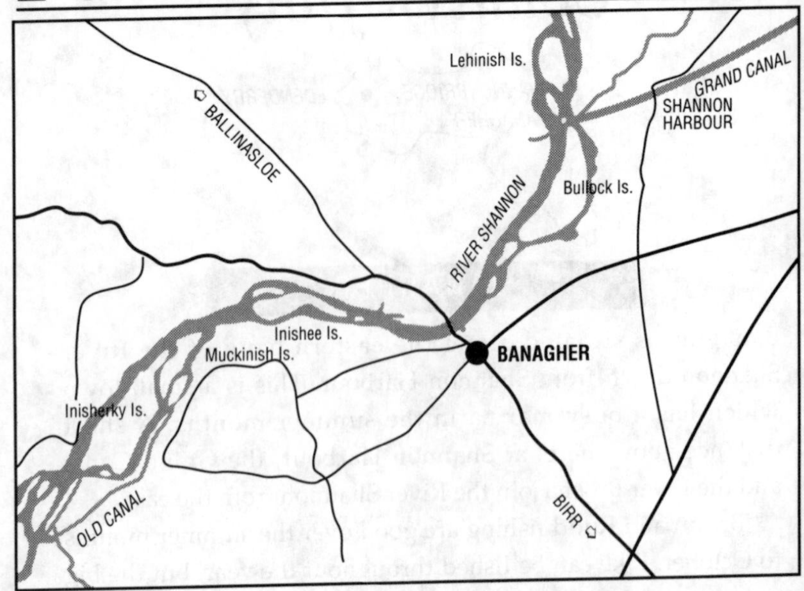

RIVER SHANNON: Above the bridge and marina, the area behind Bullock Island is excellent for all species in the early season and fishes well for Pike and Perch all year.

Down along the west bank, there are some swims for good Rudd and Perch. Near the factory, downriver and behind the island, there are some good swims for Bream.

GRAND CANAL: The canal at Shannon Harbour and farther up holds Bream, Rudd, Perch, Pike and Eels.

EDENDERRY

Edenderry is situated 32 miles west of Dublin. It is east of Tullamore on the Grand Canal. Tench and Rudd provide good sport in the summer. Bream fishing is best from mid April to October. There is a fair stock of Carp which provide good summer sport. Perch and Pike provide sport throughout the year. There are many competitions held on the Canal on different stretches.

EDENDERRY

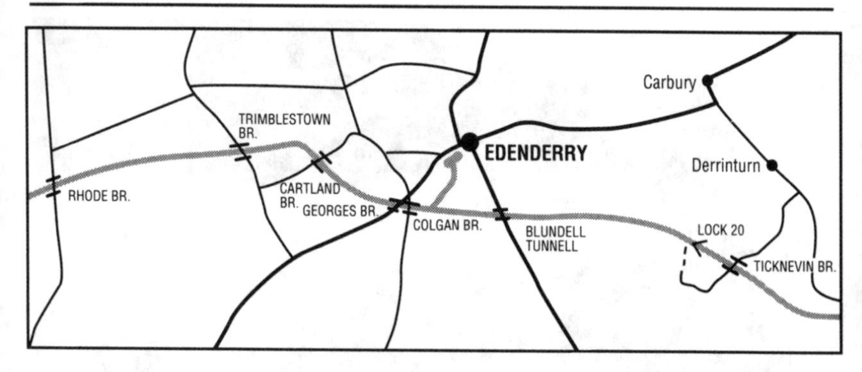

CLUB

Edenderry Angling Club, Padraic Kelly, 48 Fr Murphy Street, Edenderry, Tel (0405)32071.

ANGLING CONTACT

Padraic Kelly.

BAIT

Conlons Sports, Main Street, Edenderry, Tel (0405) 31565.

OTHER WATERS IN THIS AREA

See Enfield, Prosperous.

SPECIES

Bream, Rudd, Tench, Carp, Perch, Pike, Eels.

COMPETITION

Edenderry Festival - June

GRAND CANAL: There is a mile link to Edenderry Harbour in the town. The harbour has a good stock of Bream to 4.5 lbs and some Carp to 10 lbs. Rudd and Tench are also present. The link canal is used for matches. The main line of the canal east of Blundell Tunnel and up to Ticknevin Lock holds excellent stocks of Bream to 4 lbs, with good Tench and small Rudd. West of Trimblestown Bridge, there are good Bream to 4 lbs, with Tench to 4 lbs.

SHANNONBRIDGE

Shannonbridge is on the River Shannon and 8 miles (13 km) south of Ballinasloe on the R357 road. This is a small village down from Athlone where the River Suck joins the Shannon. Bream fishing is good from May to October. Rudd are good sport over the summer months. Tench fishing is good from early May to July and later in fine summers. Pike provide good sport all year, but the fishing for these big fish is best in the winter months. Fishing in this area is on the Rivers Shannon and Suck and also the Grand Canal. There are some small, still backwaters here.

CLUB

Shannonbridge Angling Club, Dermot Killeen, Shannonbridge, Tel (0905) 74112.

ANGLING CONTACTS

Dermot Killeen, Killeen's Pub, Tel (0905) 74112.
Guesthouse owners are experienced in dealing with anglers.

TACKLE SHOPS

Al Cunningham's, Athlone.
Jim Griffin, Tackle Shop, Rahan, Tel (0506) 55979.
Killeen's Shop, Shannonbridge, Tel (0905) 74112.

BAIT

Don Egan, Shannonview House, Athlone, Tel (0902) 4773.
D. Killeen, Killeen's Pub, Shannonbridge, Tel (0905) 74112.
Jim Griffin, Tackle Shop, Rahan, Tel (0506) 55979.

OTHER WATERS IN THIS AREA

See Ballinasloe, Athlone, Banagher.

SPECIES

Bream, Rudd, Hybrids, some Roach, Perch, Pike, Tench, Eels.

BOATS

Killeen's Pub, Shannonbridge, Tel (0905) 74112.

SHANNONBRIDGE

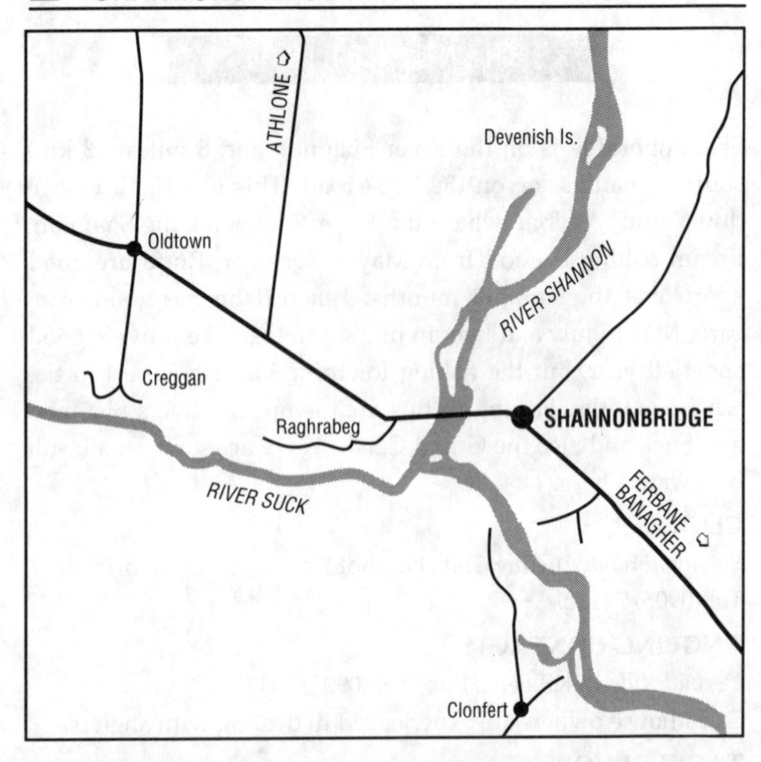

RIVER SHANNON: The river beside Shannonbridge has many good stretches for Bream to 5 lbs (2.2 kg), Rudd to 2 lbs (0.9 kg), Rudd/Bream Hybrids to 5 lbs (2.2 kg) and with some Tench to 6 lbs (2.7 kg), Perch, Pike, Eels and some Roach. Above the bridge, the island area has fast water and good Rudd. Upriver behind the island along the west bank, there is good, quiet water for Bream. Still farther upriver, behind other islands, there is good Rudd fishing and Rudd/Bream Hybrids.

Downriver at the power station in the hot water effluent, some Tench to 6 lbs (2.7 kg) and good Rudd are common. The short bank stretch here also produces good Bream fishing.

RIVER SUCK: The slow-making river at Creggan holds good Bream. Just up from the Shannon junction, there is a good stretch for Bream, Rudd, Perch, Pike, Eels and some Roach.

County Roscommon

BOYLE

Boyle is located south of the Curlew Mountains and is on the Dublin-Sligo road (N4). The town is located between Lough Gara to the west and the scenic Lough Key and has the Boyle River flowing rapidly through it.

Bream fishing is good from late April to October. Roach are present and provide good sport all year. Tench fishing is best in May and June. Pike are also in the area and give good results all year but are best in the colder months. Fishing in this area is in lakes and rivers.

CLUB

Boyle and District Angling Association, Mrs A. McGlynn, Deerpark, Boyle, Tel (079) 62455.

ANGLING CONTACTS

Hotel and guesthouse owners are experienced in dealing with anglers.

TACKLE SHOPS

Christy Wynne, Newsagent and fishing tackle.
Brian Flaherty, Abbey Marine, Carrick Road.

BAIT

M. Mitchell, Abbey House, Boyle, Tel (079) 62385.

OTHER WATERS IN THE AREA

See Carrick-on-Shannon, Drumshanbo, Strokestown.

SPECIES

Bream, Roach, Rudd, Hybrids, Perch, Pike, Tench, Eels.

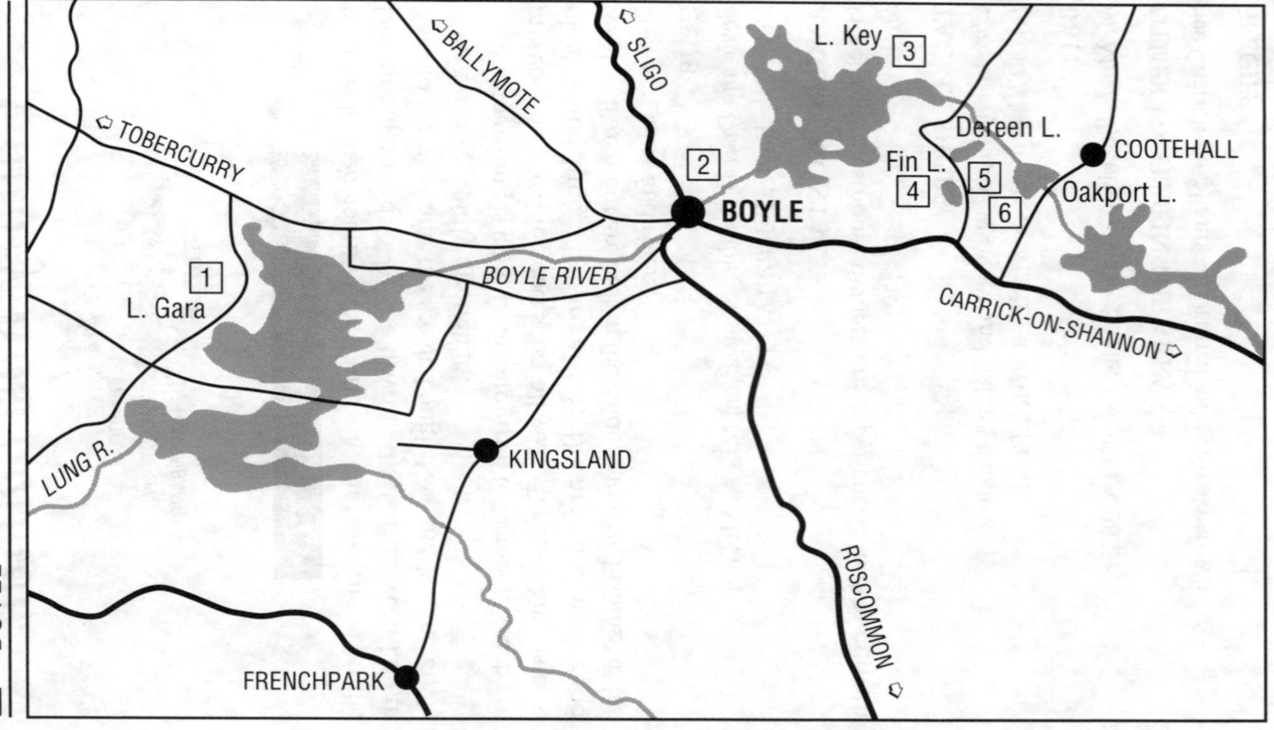
SLIGO
BALLYMOTE
TOBERCURRY
L. Key
3
2
BOYLE
Dereen L.
Fin L.
4
5
6
COOTEHALL
Oakport L.
1
L. Gara
BOYLE RIVER
CARRICK-ON-SHANNON
LUNG R.
KINGSLAND
ROSCOMMON
FRENCHPARK

MAPS

Central Fisheries Board Angling Maps – Boyle, Carrick-on-Shannon, Drumshanbo, Strokestown.

BOATS

Lough Key Forest Park, Tel (079) 67037.
Brian Flaherty, Abbey Marine, Carrick Road, Tel (079) 62053.

1. LOUGH GARA: At its entry to Lough Gara at Float, the Lung River holds good stocks of Bream. The lake itself is divided in two and in the lower section, there are some good Bream swims. The lake has Roach, Perch, Pike, Bream and Eels.
2. BOYLE RIVER: At Drum Bridge and downriver, there are big stocks of Perch. The slow-moving river has Bream, Roach, Hybrids and Pike.
3. LOUGH KEY: This big water has a good stock of coarse fish, with some good Brown Trout. It can only be fished with success from a boat. This is particularly so for Pike. Bream are to be found in the reeded bays, where Roach and Perch are also located.
4. FIN LAKE: This water is beside the Boyle-Knockvicar road and is fishable from stands. It holds Tench and the best results are at night. There are also some good Roach here.
5. DEREEN LAKE: This lake is in a forest and fishing is from stands. It produces Bream, Roach, Hybrids, Perch, Pike and Eels. Access is normally closed and a key must be obtained to enter here. See local notices.

   SHANBALLYBAN LAKE: There is good parking near this lake where fishing is from stands for Bream, Roach, Hybrids, Perch, Pike and Eels.
6. OAKPORT LAKE: This good lake on the Boyle River is at Cootehall. Approached from the bridge, the water provides excellent catches of Bream, Roach, Rudd, Hybrids, Pike and Perch. Below Cootehall Bridge there is also good fishing at the jetty.

CASTLECOOTE

Castlecoote is a small village on the R366 road from Roscommon. It lies close to the top of the River Suck and is near the county town of Roscommon. Bream and Rudd fishing are good from May to October. Pike fishing is good all year, but it is at its best in the colder months. Rudd feed in the summer months and Tench fishing is productive in May and June. Fishing here is in the River Suck and also on some lakes.

CLUB

Athleague and Fuerty Angling Club, Kieron Connell, Athleague, Tel (0903) 7869.

ANGLING CONTACTS

Guesthouse owners are experienced in dealing with anglers.

TACKLE SHOP

C.J. Finn, Roscommon.

BAIT

Don Egan, Shannonview House, Athlone, Tel (0902) 94773.

Bill Burton, 'Woodlands', Ballinasloe, Tel (0905) 43123.

Mrs Holmes, Lakeside Store, Lanesborough, Tel (043) 21491.

OTHER WATERS IN THIS AREA

See Lanesborough, Ballinasloe, Athlone.

SPECIES

Bream, Rudd, Hybrids, Perch, Pike, Tench, Eels and some Roach.

COMPETITIONS

Castlecoote Open – August

1. RIVER SUCK: The river at Donamon bridge above Castlecoote is shallow, with Perch, Rudd and Roach. Below here, the river is slow and deeper, with some shoals of good Bream to 4 lbs (1.8 kg). This area down to Castlecoote also has good Rudd to 1.5 lbs (.9 kg), with Perch, Pike and Eels.

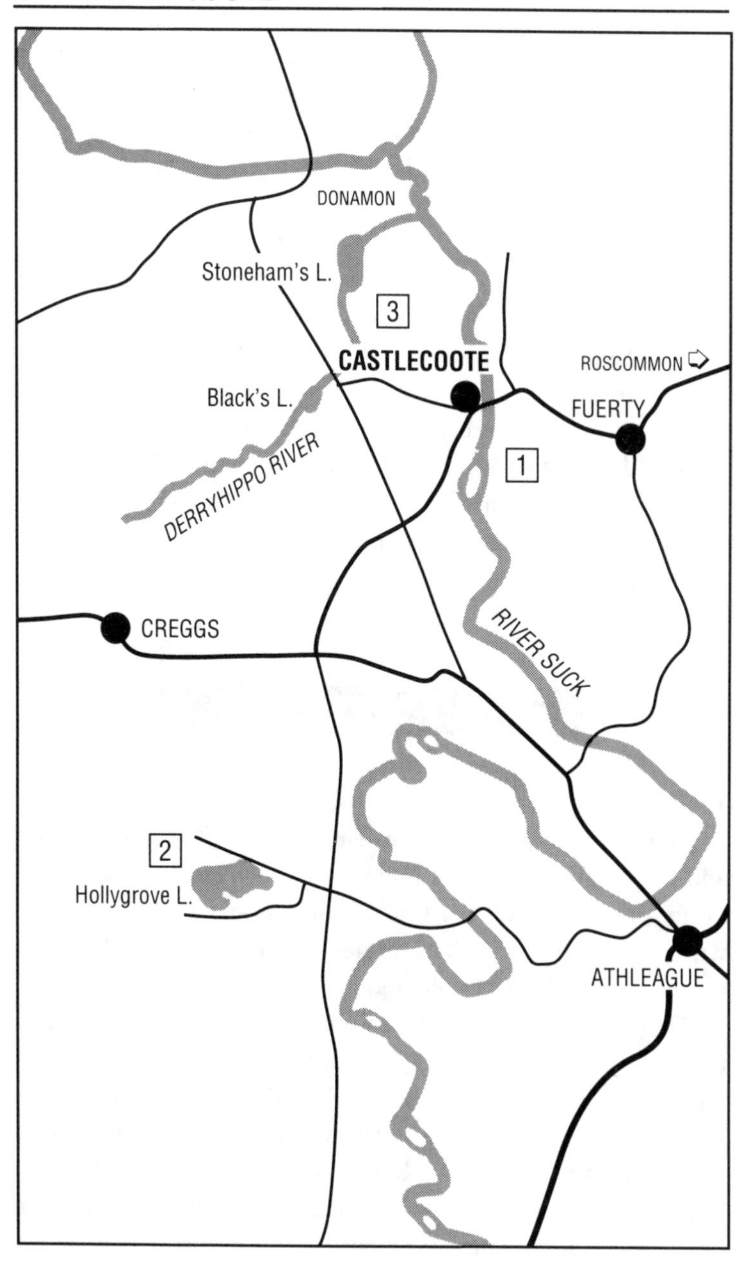
DONAMON
Stoneham's L.
3
CASTLECOOTE
ROSCOMMON
Black's L.
FUERTY
1
DERRYHIPPO RIVER
CREGGS
RIVER SUCK
2
Hollygrove L.
ATHLEAGUE

About 3 miles (4.8 km) down, beside the factory at Athleague, the river holds a fair stock of Bream, Rudd and Perch. Good Pike are common throughout this whole section on the River Suck especially the section near Ballygar and also farther down to Ballyforan Bridge.

2. HOLLYGROVE LAKE: This water is 3 miles (4.8 km) south of Castlecoote and fishes well for Tench to 6 lbs (2.7 kg). Fishing is from stands on this reeded water. On low water conditions, bank fishing is possible from the 'Island'. This lake is also near Ballygar and has good access.
3. STONEHAM'S LAKE AND BLACK'S LAKE: These waters beside the village have soft, reeded margins and the best results come from boat fishing. They offer good fishing for Rudd, with Perch and some Bream. Stoneham's Lake has a good stock of Rudd/Bream Hybrids, with Perch, Pike and Eels. It also holds a stock of quality Bream.

ROOSKY

The River Shannon divides the town of Roosky which is on the Dublin-Sligo road (N4). The west bank is in Co. Roscommon and the east bank is in Co. Longford. Roosky lies below loughs Bofin and Boderg on the River Shannon and the area is busy with cruising traffic in the summer months. Fishing in this area is in lakes and the River Shannon.

There are vast waters here with great unfished areas open for discovering good angling. Bream fishing is good from mid April to October, and good-quality Rudd feed during the summer. Tench are at their best in May and June, and Roach are good all year but give better sport in the colder months. Pike fishing is good all year round but the best months are from September to March.

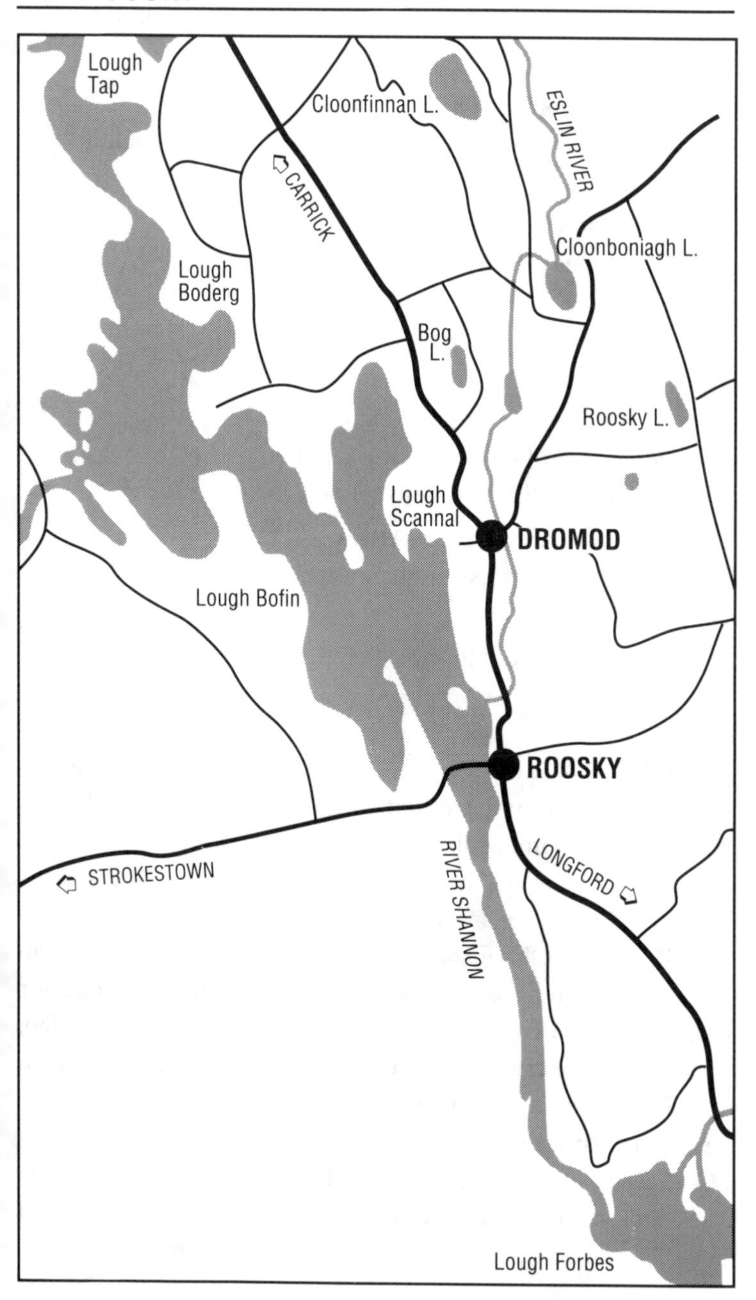
Lough Tap
Cloonfinnan L.
ESLIN RIVER
CARRICK
Cloonboniagh L.
Lough Boderg
Bog L.
Roosky L.
Lough Scannal
DROMOD
Lough Bofin
ROOSKY
LONGFORD
RIVER SHANNON
STROKESTOWN
Lough Forbes

CLUB

Lakeland Angling Club, D. Rowley, Lakeland House, Roosky, Tel (078) 38064.

ANGLING CONTACTS

Guesthouse owners in this area are experienced in dealing with anglers.

TACKLE SHOPS

M. Fox, The Quay, Roosky.

Conroy's Shop, Roosky.

The Creel, Main Street, Carrick-on-Shannon.

BAIT

Lakeland Bait Centre, Roosky, Tel (078) 38064.

Bill Boulton, Credit Union House, Dromod.

Irish Angling Bait Services, Ballyconnell, Tel (049) 26258.

OTHER WATERS IN THIS AREA

See also Mohill, Carrick-on-Shannon, Strokestown.

SPECIES

Bream, Roach, Rudd, Hybrids, Perch, Pike, Eels, Tench.

LOUGHS BODERG, BOFIN, SCANNAL: These are big Shannon lakes, heavily reeded, and fishing is best done from a boat but with some isolated swims which can be fished from the bank. These waters hold Bream, Roach, good Rudd, Hybrids, Perch, Pike and Eels.

RIVER SHANNON: Fishing above the town is from stands on the left bank and there is also some open bank. It is good for Bream, Roach, Perch, some Rudd and Pike. Below the bridge, where there are cruisers in the summer, there are Roach, Perch and Eels. There are also some good swims over the lock and below the fast weir water.

BOG LAKE: This lake, off the Longford road near Dromod, has a stock of small Tench, and also holds Roach, Perch, Pike and Eels.

STROKESTOWN

Strokestown lies west of the Shannon and is situated on the N5 road, 13 miles (20 km) west of Longford. It is a market town with wide and spacious streets. The waters in this area are famous for their clarity and they hold good-quality Rudd which feed freely in the summer months.

Bream, though not common to all waters, feed from mid April to October. There are few Roach here at this time. Pike fishing continues throughout the year and is best in the colder months. Fishing here is in a variety of lakes.

CLUB

Strokestown Angling Club, S. Sheil, Bridge Street, Strokestown, Tel (078) 33022.

ANGLING CONTACTS

Hotel and guesthouse owners are experienced in dealing with anglers.

BAIT

Mrs Homes, Lakeside Store, Lanesborough, Tel (043) 21401.
Lakeland Bait Centre, Roosky, Tel (078) 38064.
Bill Boulton, Credit Union House, Dromod.

OTHER WATERS IN THIS AREA

See Roosky, Tarmonbarry, Lanesborough.

SPECIES

Rudd, Perch, Pike, Tench, Eels and Bream.

BOATS

George Gearty, Publican, Strokestown, Tel (078) 21401.

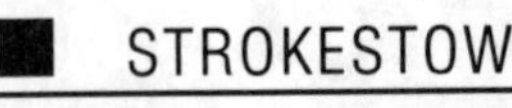

STROKESTOWN

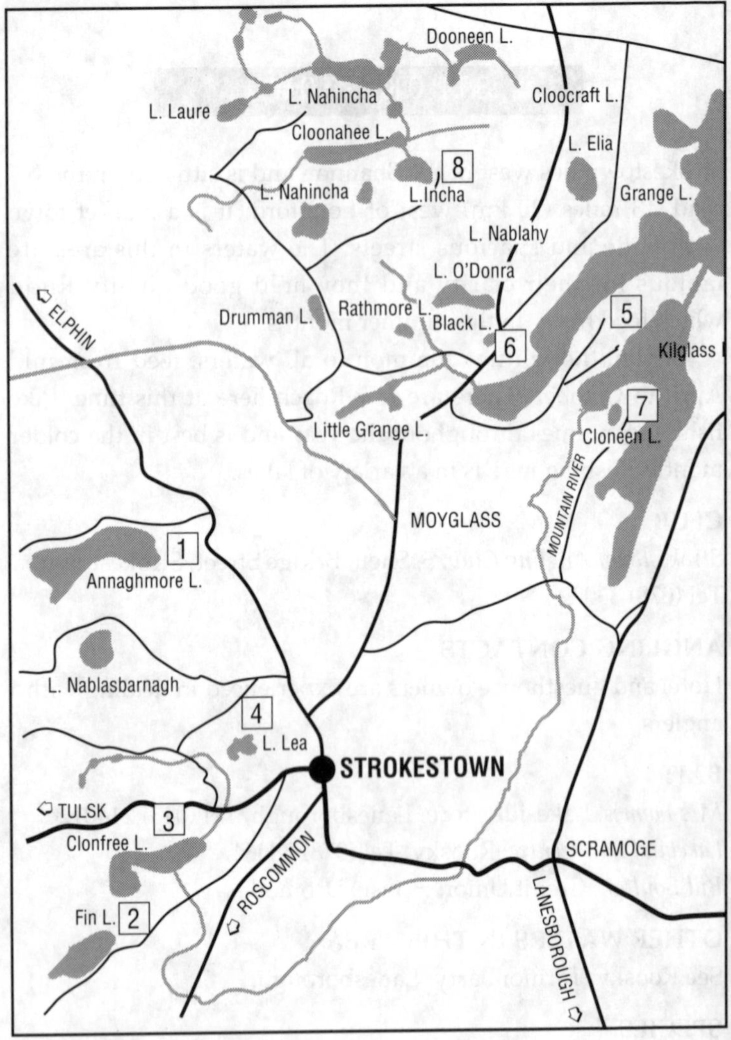

1. ANNAGHMORE LAKE: A rich lake, 3 miles (4.8 km) from Strokestown and off the Elphin road, it has shallow margins and reeds. This lake has a good stock of big Rudd to over 3 lbs (1.3 kg). It also holds Perch, some Tench and Pike.

2. FIN LAKE: Access is easy to this water which has belts of reeds. It is 2 miles (3.2 km) west of Strokestown and is fishable from stands for Rudd and Perch.
3. CLONFREE LAKE: This water, 1 mile (1.6 km) from Strokestown, is surrounded by reeds. It has good stocks of Rudd over 2 lbs (0.9 kg), Tench to 5 lbs (2.2 kg) and also holds some Brown Trout.
4. LOUGH LEA: These are several small ponds with connecting streams near the town. Fishing is from stands for Perch to 2 lbs (0.9 kg), Rudd and some Bream. It also fishes for Tench in May and June.
5. GRANGE AND KILGLASS LAKES: These lakes fringed with reeds hold big stocks of good Rudd to 3 lbs (1.3 kg). The waters also have a fair stock of Bream and Rudd/Bream Hybrids, with Perch, Pike, Eels and also some Roach. Fishing is from stands in some places.
6. BLACK LAKE: This is a small water with a fair stock of small Tench, with Rudd and Perch.
7. CLONEEN LAKE: A reeded water, fishing is from stands for Tench to 4 lbs (1.8 kg), with Rudd, Perch and Pike.
8. LOUGH INCHA: A small water with easy waterside parking. It holds Rudd and some Rudd/Bream Hybrids, with Perch and Pike.

TARMONBARRY

Tarmonbarry is west of the River Shannon in Co. Roscommon, while its neighbouring village of Clondara on the eastern bank is in Co. Longford. These villages are situated on the N5 road between Longford and Strokestown.

The River Shannon is wide here and there is a weir and lock below the village. There is also a short canal, and the rivers Feorish and Camlin enter the Shannon here. Bream fishing is best between May and October. Roach are common and feed best in the colder months. Tench fishing, though limited, is good in May and June, and Pike fishing is all year but the colder months produce the best results. The main fishing here is in the River Shannon, but there are also lakes and the rivers Camlin and Feorish.

CLUB

None.

ANGLING CONTACT

Barry Keenan, Public House, Tarmonbarry, Tel (043) 26098.

BAIT

Lakeland Bait Centre, Roosky.

Barry Keenan, Shannonside Guesthouse, Tarmonbarry, Tel (043) 26052.

Bill Boulton, Credit Union House, Dromod.

Mrs Holmes, Lakeside Store, Lanesborough, Tel (043) 21491.

OTHER WATERS IN THIS AREA

See Strokestown, Roosky, Lanesborough.

SPECIES

Bream, Rudd, Roach, Hybrids, Perch, Pike, Eels, Tench.

BOATS

Barry Keenan, Shannonside, Tarmonbarry, Tel (043) 26052.

TARMONBARRY

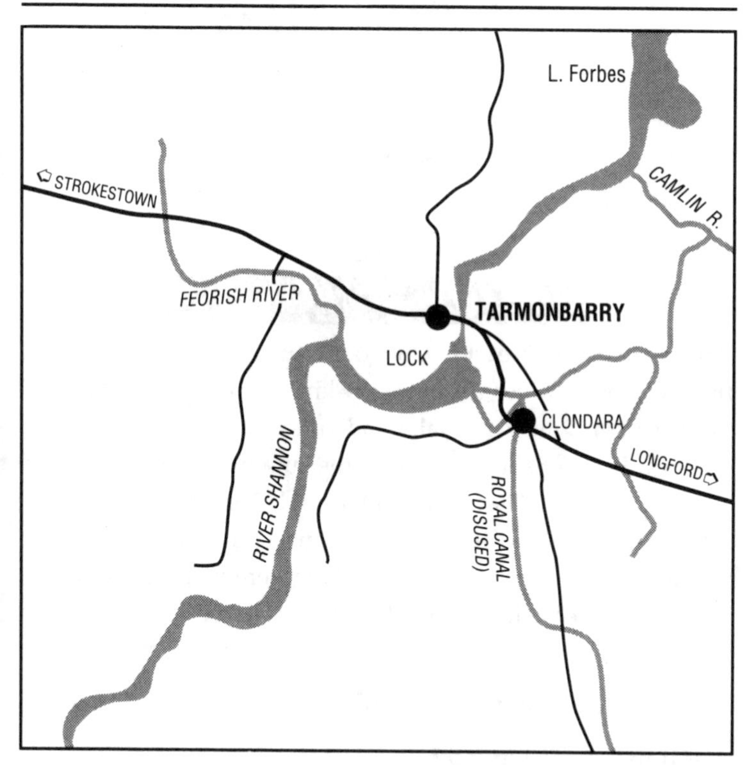

RIVER SHANNON: Above the bridge, the river is fast and heavily reeded. There are some swims for Bream and Roach. Below the weir and along the left bank, there is a channel where fishing is good for Roach and Bream. Farther down, there is good bank fishing at Kilnacarrow bridge.

RIVER FEORISH: This river is slow and often weedy and holds small Bream, Roach, Perch, some Tench and Eels.

CAMLIN RIVER: A quiet river with good banks, this water produces Bream, Roach, Perch and Tench, with Pike and Eels.

County Sligo

BALLYMOTE

Ballymote in south-east Co. Sligo is situated near the waters of the Owenmore River, 15 miles (24 km) from Sligo. It is a small market town which has lake and river coarse fishing nearby. The best Bream fishing is during the summer, when Rudd and Tench also feed. The waters also hold Perch, Pike and Eels. Pike fishing is good in the winter and early spring, but Pike will feed throughout the year. Fishing here is mostly in lakes, with some river fishing in the Owenmore River.

CLUB

Ballymote Development Association.

ANGLING CONTACTS

Padraic Judge, Castle House, Ballymote.
Sandy Perceval, Templehouse, Ballymote, Tel (071) 83329.

TACKLE SHOPS

See Carrick-on-Shannon and Boyle.

BAIT

See Carrick-on-Shannon and Boyle.

OTHER WATERS IN THIS AREA

See Boyle, Carrick-on-Shannon.

SPECIES

Bream, Rudd, Roach, Pike, Perch, Eels.

BOAT

S. Perceval, Templehouse, Tel (071) 83329.

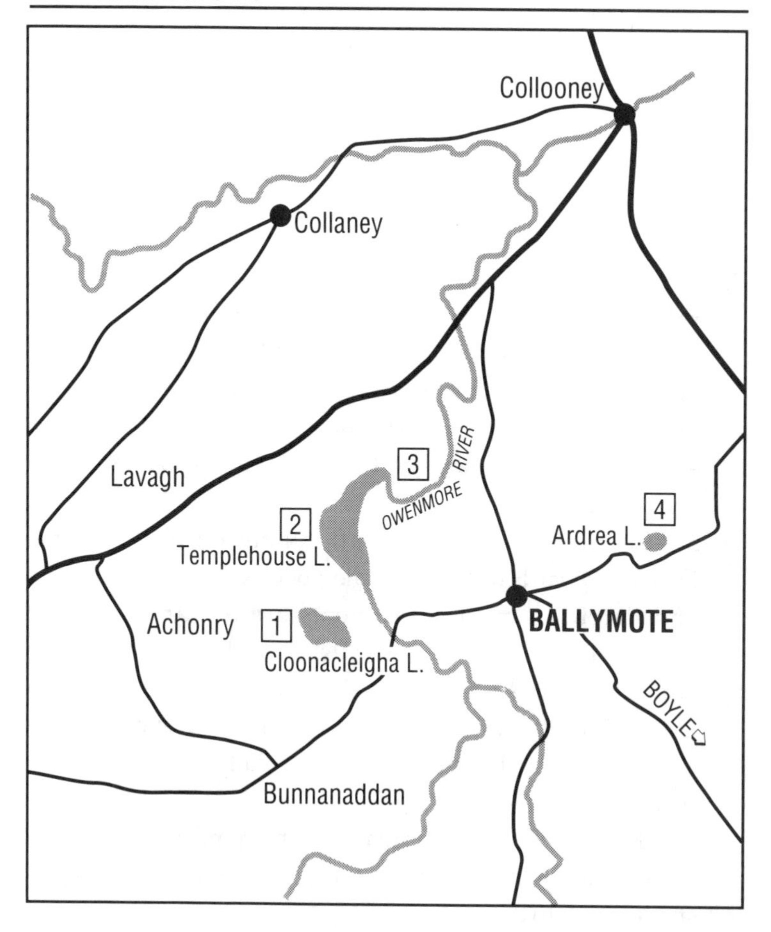

1. CLOONACLEIGHA LAKE: This lake has a thick belt of reeds and drains into Templehouse Lake. There are some peaty margins and some firm ground where it can be shallow. In general, this is a shallow water which in summer has much weed. Fishing is mostly from a boat. The water provides good sport for good-sized Perch and Pike. There are also some Bream, Rudd and Eels.
2. TEMPLEHOUSE LAKE: This lake is on the Owenmore River. It can boast of its stock of good-quality Pike. Reeded

in most places, fishing on this water is best from a boat. It also holds Bream, Rudd, Hybrids, Perch and Eels. The access to one section of Templehouse Lake is over private lands.

3. OWENMORE RIVER: This slow-making river has some deep pools which hold Bream, mostly in the early season. The river, with clean open banks, provides sport for Rudd, Perch, Pike and Eels.
4. ARDREA LAKE: This small lake has easy access from the road where fishing is from stands. In this water, there are Tench, some Bream, Rudd, Perch and Pike.

LOUGH GILL: This is a very scenic 3,300 acre lake beside Sligo town. It holds good stocks of Bream, with Rudd, Pike and Perch, particularly at Hazelwood, Doonee, Kilmore and Annagh.

Special note: Within the area of the North-Western Regional Fisheries Board, there are some good waters holding Pike and Perch. In most cases, boats are required for best results. The waters near Castlebar and Ballyhaunis are better known as Castlebar Lakes, Levally Lake, Guiltybo Lake, Manulla Lake, Carrowmore Lake, Derryhick Lake, Caheer Lake and Eaton's Lake near Ballyhaunis in which there are some Bream.

LAKEHILL POND: This small water 1.5 miles from Knock has easy access from the road. It produces great catches of small Tench to 3 lbs.

County Waterford

CAPPOQUIN

Cappoquin is a small town on the N72, 20 miles east of Fermoy on the River Blackwater at the top of the tidal waters. The freshwater here is backed up by the tide and fishing is best when the water is either rising or falling. Roach and Dace fishing is good throughout the year, but they are at their best in the autumn and spring.

CLUB

Cappoquin Angling Club, Jim Wall, Kilbree House, Cappoquin.

ANGLING CONTACTS

Guesthouse owners in this area are experienced in dealing with anglers.

Mossy Noonan, Toby Jug Inn, Cappoquin.

TACKLE SHOP

Mary Fives, Jewellers, Main Street, Cappoquin.

BAIT

Evelyn Flynn, River View House, Cook Street, Cappoquin, Tel (058) 54073.

OTHER WATERS IN THIS AREA

See Fermoy.

SPECIES

Roach, Dace, Eels, Perch, some Pike, Tench.

CAPPOQUIN

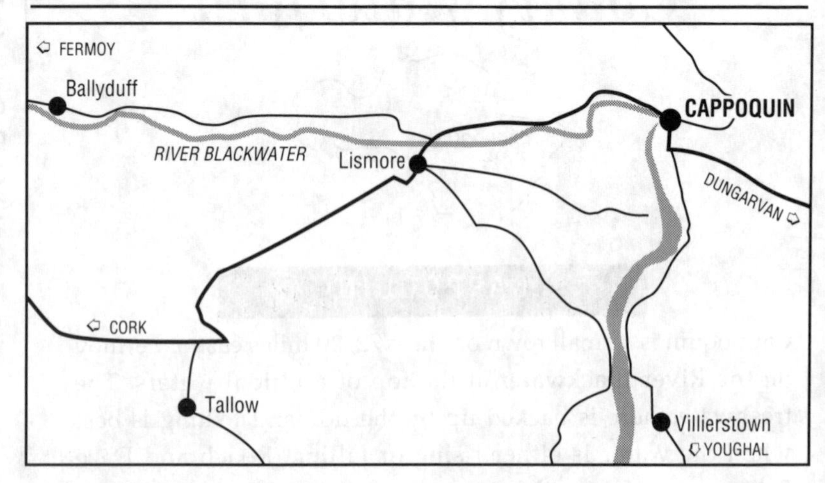

RIVER BLACKWATER: The river is tidal here and this movement of water affects the fishing. Shoals of good Roach and Dace are located in many sections of the river where access is good.

Special Note: The River Blackwater is a mixed fishery, holding Salmon and Trout. Fishing for coarse fish is controlled by the Cappoquin Coarse Angling Club by arrangement with Lismore Estates. Coarse anglers must note that fishing is restricted to the area between the Trageen (Glenribbon Bridge) to the lay-by on the Youghal Road along both banks.

Coarse fishing permit (£3.00 per week) is available from Jim Wall or Mrs Evelyn Flynn.

DROMANA LAKE: This is a small private water which holds small Rudd and Tench.

County Westmeath

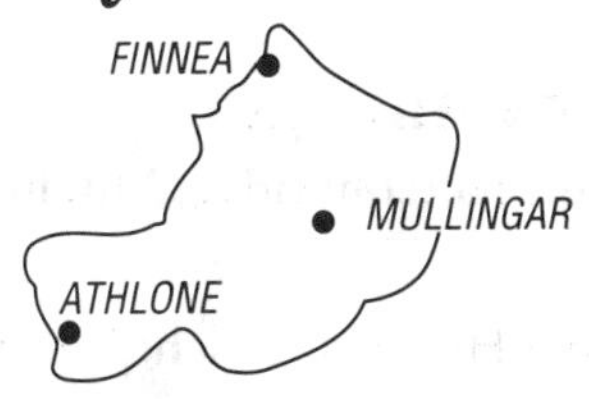

ATHLONE

Athlone, on the River Shannon, is located on the Dublin-Galway road (N6). This is a big, industrious town in the centre of the country. It boasts good facilities such as golf, tennis, swimming and marinas. The River Shannon leaving Lough Ree flows through the town and dominates the whole area.

In the early months, the river Bream are slow to feed. As the summer progresses, the massive shoals give great sport right into October. Rudd feed freely in the summer, while the Roach feed all year. Pike fishing continues all year. Perch are in abundance over most of the season.

CLUB

Athlone Tourist Development Association, Mrs Nancy Denby, Shelmalier House, Cartontroy, Retreat Road, Athlone, Tel (0902) 72245.

ANGLING CONTACTS

Don Egan, Shannonside House, West Lodge Road, Athlone, Tel (0902) 94773.

Al Cunningham, Tackle Shop, Riverside, Athlone.

Hotel and guesthouse owners are experienced in dealing with anglers.

TACKLE SHOPS

Don Egan, Shannonside House, West Lodge Road, Athlone, Tel (0902) 94773.

The Hooker Tackle Shop, Athlone.

Al Cunningham, Tackle Shop, Riverside.

BAIT

Don Egan, Shannonside House, West Lodge Road, Athlone, Tel (0902) 94773.

OTHER WATERS IN THIS AREA

See also Ballinasloe, Shannonbridge, Mullingar.

SPECIES

Bream, Rudd, Roach, Hybrids, Tench, Perch, Pike, Eels.

COMPETITIONS

Festival – July and October.

■ ATHLONE

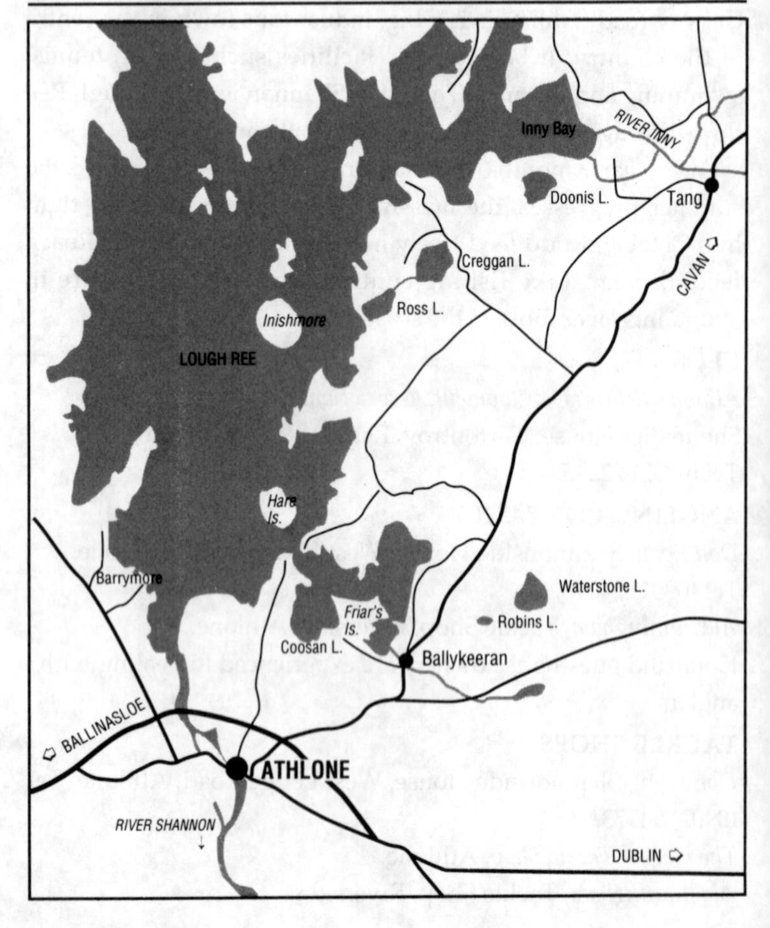

LOUGH REE: This is a big and rich water with an abundance of big coarse fish, including Bream to 11 lbs (4.9 kg), Rudd to 3 lbs (1.3 kg), Rudd/Bream Hybrids to 7 lbs (3.1 kg), Roach, Perch, Pike, Eels and good-quality Tench.

The lake can be fished at isolated places where there is good bank and good fishing depth. However, most places are accessible from a boat only.

The Inner Lakes at Ballykeeran along the Longford road are worth a try for Tench, Roach and Rudd.

The Inny Bay, approached from Tang, holds big stocks of Bream and Rudd/Bream Hybrids in the early season.

The River Inny at the Red Bridge down from Ballymahon is a good fishery for Roach, Bream, Hybrid with Perch, Pike and some Brown Trout.

Along the western shore at Ballymore, which is approached off the Roscommon road, there is a good stretch for all species. There are some good swims above the caravan park at Hodson Bay.

RIVER SHANNON: The river above the town railway bridge has good Rudd to 2 lbs (0.9 kg), with a lot of Perch and Roach. Below the town, the river has a big stock of Bream (average size 3.5 lbs/1.5 kg) with Perch, Rudd, Roach and Eels. The Meadows and Burgess park stretches here are used for matches, when good catches are recorded. Farther down, there are other stretches which still retain quality fishing, where Roach are now appearing in numbers. Stocks of Pike and Perch are good throughout, but more particularly farther downriver.

FINNEA

Finnea is located on the Cavan-Mullingar road (R394) almost midway between the two towns. It is a small village between Co. Cavan and Co. Westmeath and is near the game fishing at Lough Sheelin.

CLUBS

Finnea Development Association.
Mullingar CAC, Joe Gavin, Tel (044) 42147.

ANGLING CONTACTS

Sean Gurhy, Shannon Regional Fisheries Board, Kilnahard, Mullaghboy, Tel (049) 36144.
Matt Nolan, Shannon Regional Fisheries Board, Tel (044) 48769.

BAIT

O'Malley's, Dominick Street, Mullingar, Tel (044) 48300.
Sam's Tackle Shop, Castle Street, Mullingar, Tel (044) 40431.

TACKLE SHOP

O'Malley's, Dominick Street, Mullingar.
Sam's Tackle Shop, Castle Street, Mullingar, Tel (044) 40431.

OTHER WATERS IN THIS AREA

See Cavan, Gowna, Multyfarnham and Mullingar.

SPECIES

Roach, Perch, Bream, Hybrids, Pike.

BOATS

Stephen Reilly, Innyside Guest House, Finnea, Tel (043) 81124.

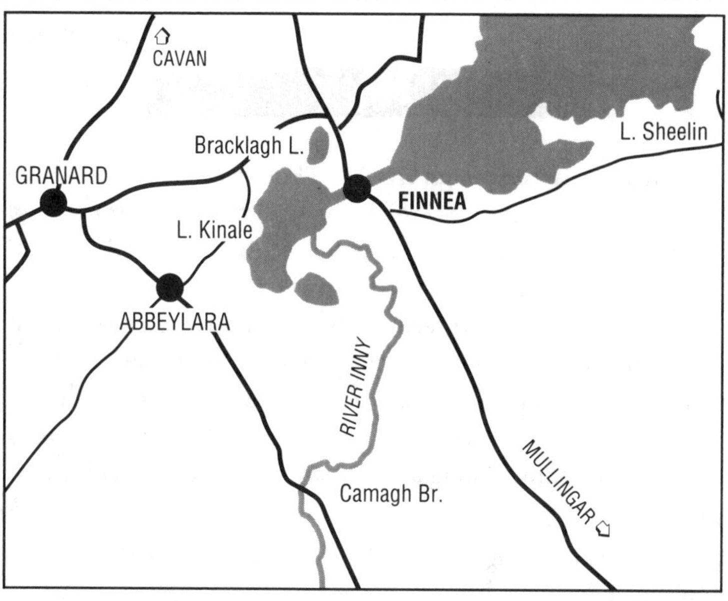

RIVER INNY: The River Inny down from the bridge is fast. During the period from late September to late April, it holds good stocks of quality Roach. In the summer, the river is often shallow and weedy. Winter fishing, down from the bridge, offers excellent fishing for Roach to 1.5 lbs (0.6 kg), some Bream and good Hybrids to 2 lbs (0.9 kg) when the water is cloudy.

LOUGH KINALE: A big water, through which the River Inny flows. A reeded water, it is best fished from a boat which can be brought down from the slip at Finnea. It holds a good stock of Pike and good Roach. It also holds some Bream, Rudd, Hybrids, Perch and Eels.

MULLINGAR

Mullingar, between Lough Owel and Lough Ennell, is located on the Dublin-Longford (N4) road, about 50 miles (80 km) west of Dublin. It is a large and prosperous town, situated in good farming country. The disused Royal Canal runs through the town. Bream and Rudd feed freely from mid April to October. Roach are at their best in the colder months, but are available for most of the year. Pike fishing is good throughout the year, while Tench fishing is at its best in May and June. Fishing here is mostly in lakes, with some fishing in the canal and also the River Inny.

CLUB

Mullingar Coarse Angling Club, P. McConville, Springfield, Mullingar.

ANGLING CONTACTS

Matt Nolan, Shannon Regional Fisheries Board, Mullingar, Tel (044) 48769.

Joe Gavin, Mullingar Coarse Fishing Club, (044) 42147.

Hotel and guesthouse owners are experienced in dealing with anglers.

TACKLE SHOPS

O'Malley's, 33 Dominick Street, Mullingar, Tel (044) 48300.

Sam Smith, Sam's Tackle Shop, Castle Street, Mullingar, Tel (044) 40431.

BAIT

O'Malley's, 33 Dominick Street, Tel (044) 48300.

Sam Smith, Sam's Tackle Shop, Castle Street, Mullingar, Tel (044) 40431.

WATERS FISHED

Lakes and rivers.

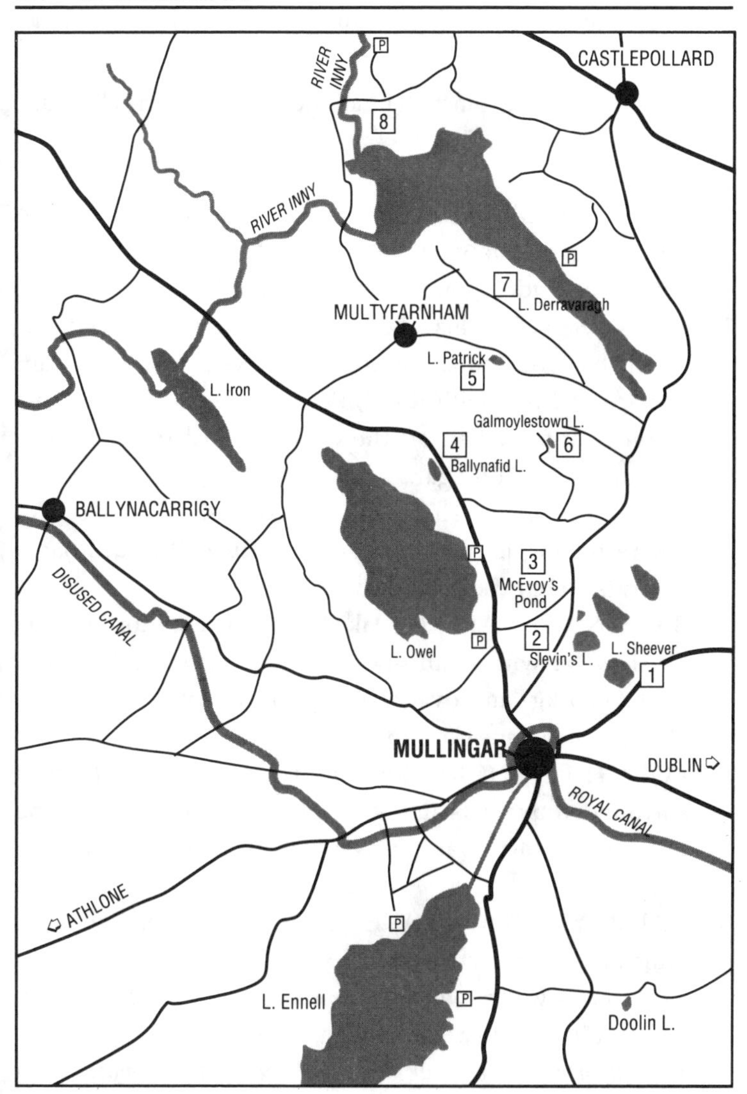

OTHER WATERS IN THIS AREA

See also Finnea, Athlone.

SPECIES

Bream, Rudd, Roach, Hybrids, Tench, Perch, Carp, Pike, Eels.

MAPS

Central Fisheries Board Maps – Mullingar/River Inny, Athlone.

BOATS

For Lough Patrick, contact Shannon Regional Fisheries Board, Mullingar, Tel (044) 48769.

1. LOUGH SHEEVER: Access to this water is over private ground near the town. It holds good Bream to 6 lbs (2.7 kg), with some Rudd, Roach, Perch, Pike and Eels.
2. SLEVIN'S LAKE: This lake is rich and has much weed, but is fishable from stands. It holds some good-quality Bream to 5 lbs (2.2 kg), with Rudd, Perch and some Roach. This water is approached off the Castlepollard road, 2 miles (3.2 km) from Mullingar.
3. McEVOY'S POND: This is a small lake beside Slevin's Lake where fishing is from stands. It produces Rudd, Roach, Hybrids, Perch, Tench and some Carp.
4. BALLYNAFID LAKE: The lake beside the Longford road is a rich water with small stocks of specimen-sized Bream to 10 lbs (4.5 kg) and over. This water also produces Rudd, Hybrids and some Carp to 13 lbs (5.8 kg).
5. LOUGH PATRICK: This lake near Multyfarnham is surrounded by reeds and is fished from boats which can be hired locally. The water has a good stock of Tench to 5 lbs (2.2 kg).
6. GALMOYLESTOWN LAKE: This is a small, shallow pond which has a good stock of Carp to 12 lbs (5.4 kg). Access is easy to this water, which is approached off the Mullingar-Castlepollard road at Taughman church.

   It is important to remember that fish must not be removed from this water.
7. LOUGH DERRAVARAGH: This is a big and deep water which holds Brown Trout. It is fished for Roach from September to April. The lake also has good-quality Pike, mostly taken from a boat, but is also fishable from the shore.

8. RIVER INNY: Above Lough Derravaragh at Coolnagun Bridge, there is good fishing for Roach in the colder months of the year. Rudd and Hybrids are also present. Roach are also taken at the Inny Bridge below Lough Derravaragh.

DYSART LAKES, DELVIN: Lough Analla is the largest of a string of lakes, which lie 4 km south-west of Delvin town and which cover an area approximately 12 hectares. The lakes are signposted from the Delvin to Mullingar road, and there is foot access to the fishery from the small car park. The lake margins are reeded and angling is difficult, but the Dysart Lakes hold big stocks of Roach, and large Rudd. The lakes, which have a good growth of lilies and Canadian Pondweed, have depths of up to 4m. The lakes also hold some good Tench with Pike and Perch.